DIRTY
FAN
MALE

a
life
in
rude
letters

xxxxxxxxxxxxxxxxxxxxxxxx

Jonny Trunk

About The Author
XXXXXXXXXXXXXXXXXXXXXX XXXXXXX
XXXXXXXXXXXXXXXXXXXXXXXX

JONNY TRUNK is a young man of diverse pursuits: collector, composer, broadcaster, DJ, a curator and the man responsible for saving some of the best film and TV music ever made for posterity via his record label, Trunk Records. He has the only dedicated soundtrack radio show in the UK and sources music for TV and film. Jonny worked in advertising for a few years before realising that it wasn't for him, and spent a few years subsequent to that working at Portobello antiques market where he picked up an encyclopaedic knowledge of erotic art and ephemera. He is currently working on a box set of *Bod*, and lists his hobbies as 'whatever I can do next'.

The names of all correspondents have been changed where necessary

HarperCollins*Entertainment*
An Imprint of HarperCollins*Publishers*
77–85 Fulham Palace Road,
Hammersmith, London W6 8JB

www.harpercollins.co.uk

Published by HarperCollins*Entertainment* 2005

1

A CIP catalogue record for this book is available from the British Library

ISBN 0 00 720772 7

Set in Stempel Garamond

Printed and bound in Italy by Lego Spa

Designed by Estuary English

Dedication[1] *and Acknowledgements*[2]

XXXXXXXXXXXXXXXXXXXXXXX XXXXXXXXXX
XXXXXXXXXXXXXXXXXXXXXXXXXXXXXX XXXXXXXXXXX

1) This book is for my dead dad.

2) There are several people who must be thanked: Eve and Big Dave for all their help and permissions, The Piglet for absolutely everything, Mother for saving letters, the dynamic Wisbey duo, The Alan Cox, Devious and Dirty Derek Collie, Alexis P, Will H, Kate Haldane for introducing me to Primark and for all her support, and of course all the other ladies at AHA, the Smallfish Massive, Tony Lyons for his patience, Ben Dunn, Brian Logan, The Beast, the magical Pee Wee Williams, Danny Baker, Graham Robertson, BBC London Live, Zoe Quick, Ted at The Warehouse, Maddy Costa, Martin Green, Damon and Steve at Fuel, Ethan Reid, Hayley Willis, Barry 7, Lara and the Whoopee Girls, Johnny and Sarah Siese, Billy at Rough Trade, Rob Fitzpatrick, Pru, Warren at the WMC, Jon Ronson, Rae Baker and George, Pascal Wise, Reeds, Helen and Andy, Tim and Amy Hebden who cannot help themselves, Emma Gooding and oh and if you've been missed from this list then I'm really very sorry and somehow I will make it up to you. Well maybe. Oh and of course anyone who dared buy and then enthused about the CD or came to see the show and spread the word.

1

IT ALL BEGAN in the boozer. A good boozer, The Cat's Back in Putney. It's in a funny place, in an industrial estate in Putney just by the Thames. You'd never know it was there. It has a curious ambience, maybe just because of the owners, possibly because of the confused furniture they've collected, maybe because of the intoxicating liquor they serve if you ask nicely very late at night. It was the occasion of a friend's birthday. We always go there on birthdays and other special occasions. You don't want to spoil a good pub. Everyone was drinking lots and talking even more. For months I had despised my job. Really hated it. I was an Advertising Copywriter. Well that was my title. It was supposed to be a creative job, I was supposed to be a creative person, but none of this seemed apparent any more.

I went for the job because I wanted to write good copy, conceive different ways of advertising, just make great adverts that would work and that I'd be proud of. But it's a shit business. I'd realised there is very little creativity. What little there is, is borrowed from other more creative fields, like movies and books. And when a good idea or script is actually created, it is then tampered with by everyone else involved: the creative director, the director, the marketing director, everyone.

So I hated the work. And I hated my boss, an arrogant, intelligent twat who collects models of tanks and pictures of himself on real ones. He'd done well in advertising as a young man, he could talk the talk. He'd then started out on his own and was happy writing what he called '2 Cs in a K' style advertising, that's an acronym of sorts for 'Two C**ts in a Kitchen'. It's simple and safe, you write TV adverts with two people discussing the benefits of the product you're selling and they are normally standing in the kitchen doing so. I also hated his attitude to creative thought or rather my creative way of working. I'd get in late every day, but the night before I'd be burning the midnight oil and working on my adverts late into the night, which is always when my best work comes out. But you can't work like that as far as the big boss is concerned, creative work must be done between 8.30 a.m. and 6.30 p.m. We were never really going to get along.

All this kind of venom was pouring out of me that very night in Putney. I was grizzling to an old mate known as 'The Beast' because of his uncanny resemblance to Aleister Crowley, London's legendary black magician and sex fiend. I'd always seen The Beast as a mentor, someone whose advice I'd always listened hard to, and nearly always adhered to. He immediately understood my hatred for and desperation with my job because he works in the movie business. And there was one final major problem – my partner. If you are a copywriter in the world of advertising, you work with an Art Director as part of a 'creative team'. It's also referred to as a marriage. I didn't hate my Art Director, he was just a very strange man. I'll admit to having my own eccentric moments but my Art Director came from another, stranger place.

We'd met at college and teamed up. He was different then; once we got a job things changed a bit. Or maybe they didn't change. He wore the same outfit to work for four years, cycling shorts and a plain blue T-shirt. He wore the same cycling shoes every day too, the sort of cycling shoes with cleats in the bottom, that are for cycling, and not for walking or working in. His life was like clockwork, he was never late, his diet regular and analysed into kilojoules and kilocalories on a weekly basis. He used to analyse samples of human poo and wee in a lab. At least he did until he discovered he could draw and that advertising was possibly a more exciting option.

He was a fine draughtsman, but advertising is not about how well you draw, so he'd spend a day drawing a layout that the creative director would then hate. He had his moments of bizarre thought too, which I found exciting and inspirational, but these popped out all too slowly for my impatient liking. However, most of our creative life together was hideous and mentally draining; he'd spend most of the day in silence as I rattled off endless rubbish and attempted to kick-start him into talking about the brief in hand. When he did talk it was normally in the character of Paul Daniels, the tiny magician. We went out together about twice in four years; his social skills had never developed, and the girls in the office were suspicious of his almost kinky silences. So there I was, with a job, a tiny salary, working for a shit company, working with a total mindfuck, hating it all and still seeing no way out.

But that night at The Cat's Back my thought patterns were changing. The Beast speaks in his clear, concise lisp: 'You have to leave, Jonny. Juth leave. Fuck it all. Juth get the fuck out. How much worth could it be? What have you got to looth?'

The more he spits out these simple instructions the more exciting the prospect becomes. The alcohol makes me feel excited by it all, even a little brave for once. 'Yeah, fuck it all, I'm young, nothing could be worse than this. Yeah, fuck it all. I'll leave tomorrow.'

The Beast is insistent and goading. 'You'll never leave, Jonny. You don't have the gutth.'

'Yes I do!'

The argument continues well into the night.

I finally get to bed. I don't sleep. I think about what would happen if I stay. I think about what could happen if I leave.

In the morning I storm into work early for once, tell my partner what's going on, and hand in my notice. My partner hands in his notice too, which I find entertaining. There's a vague attempt by the boss to get us to stay, but I think we all knew what was really going on.

Leaving your job with no job to go to may sound foolish, but I really can't recommend it highly enough. The elation, the feelings of freedom and excitement that flow about you for days are almost too much to bear. My four weeks' notice fly by, and when my leaving day finally arrives we throw the best party that small grotty agency has ever had, much to the disapproval of the head man. The proceedings are somewhat enhanced by a gentleman called Sebastian. He's a gay stoner who lives 10 yards from the agency and has proved himself an entertaining distraction on the occasional evening after work. He claims to be one of David Lean's last-ever lovers, and lives in a central London council flat done up like a Victorian country house, complete with a trophy room decorated with giant turtle shells and tribal shields. In the corner is a small desktop shrine to David Lean that includes his fountain pen, glasses and a charming portrait of the auteur.

For the leaving do, not only does Sebastian turn up topless, he also brings a tray full of hash cookies, straight from the *Alice B. Toklas Cookbook*. I leave the agency for the last time singing 'Everybody's Talkin'' from *Midnight Cowboy* very loudly with Vincent, the only person I really liked in the whole agency.

The best leaving do leads to the most phenomenal hangover the next morning. Then the phone rings. It's my sister.

2

I COME FROM a family that communicates rarely. Well, I communicate rarely with them. But it's great to hear from my big sister. She has recently become a porn star. Deep down I think she always wanted to be one. When she was about 16 (and fresh out of convent school) she'd got a few topless glamour shots done without my mother knowing. Mother hates anything with even a whiff of rudeness, and the discovery of these photos had caused a meltdown in the family home. My sister went to work in a bookshop in our home town of Aldershot instead, a town that is also home to the British Army.

Once there she quickly found that the shop's best-selling title was *The Joy of Sex*, a title consistently bought by the Gurkhas stationed up the road.

My sister is a great-looking girl, and soon attracted the attentions of a local boy done good. I never liked her boyfriend. He threatened me in a really cheesy fashion just after he started going out with her, and I never forgave him. I still don't know what it was all about. Anyway, they had been together for years, then got married in a registry office, had no wedding party apart from a small buffet of Marks & Spencer's nibbles, and he left her a year to the day later for drugs and another woman. Twat. He also left my sister saddled with an enormous debt, a debt she was blissfully unaware of until the divorce proceedings had concluded. He'd got a little too greedy in the housing boom of the 80s and 90s and had got buggered with negative equities. My sister had no idea she'd been made legally responsible for the mortgages. Well, that's how I'd interpreted the story. Now with all this debt she had to make money fast.

She moved back home, became one of those pretty girls who gives away fags at the airport, worked double shifts and then finally decided to do what she'd always wanted to do and become a glamour model.

She'd invented a porn name, not by combining her first pet's name and mother's address (which would have re-christened her Big Chief Cranmore), but by uniting our granny's name and her ex-husband's and rearranging the letters. So, Eve Vorley, Porn Model, was born and, fired on by the need for vengeance over her evil ex and a keen desire to make money, became successful fast.

Within weeks she was on Page 3 lying about her age, before slipping into the pages and then, not long after, on to the covers of all the top-shelf titles. She'd also broken into the editorials of the *Sport* newspaper and had become the latest favourite of both the editors and the proprietor, David Sullivan. With such powerful new friends her star was rising fast and via the newspaper had begun to receive regular fan mail. The Official Eve Vorley Fan Club was quickly born with a PO Box address in Aldershot, and Eve began to advertise and plug the club whenever she appeared in the *Sport*.

The deal for new fans was simple – you send in your £20 for the Official Eve Vorley Membership Pack and in return you get full annual membership, a couple of signed 10" x 8" colour glossy photos of Eve (one topless, one a little racier), a glossy rude mag, regular unglossy newsletters and Fan Club updates, very special offers, and to top it all an explicit Eve Vorley video. The video was unusual in that there were no moving images on it all, just still photos of my sister that would change every few minutes. Very exciting. And the fans loved it. With the Fan Club regularly advertised it began to gather momentum, and she found that her now-busy model schedule left her just too busy to deal with it all.

She 'needed a little help once a week' is what she said on the phone to her unemployed brother. The work would take, at most, one day a week, more likely a fortnight, whenever she needed a helping and willing pair of hands. Instantly I realised that this offered me an opportunity to pay my rent or at least contribute to it while still giving me lots of time in which to work out exactly what I wanted to do with the rest of my life.

So I took the job, and now once every week or fortnight I am working in porn. Very soft porn, but porn all the same. The work is simple, and involves putting membership packs together, writing names on envelopes, going to the post office buying stamps, and a trip to the sweety shop at lunchtime. My sister and I both like sweets, but the sweety shop in Grayshot where my sister is now based is a little different from all the others I'd been into for a while. Not only do they sell old-fashioned sweets by the quarter, they also run a mean range of lunchtime pies and seasonal soups, all homemade and delicious. On the way to the sweety shop there's a typical Surrey charity shop, all cricket whites and posh books. On my first visit I managed to secure a vintage DJ for a tenner which fits like a glove and I'll never wear it but that's not the point.

At the end of a working day it's my job to take the sports bags full of mail to the little local post office. This is a nightmare for a number of reasons:

1) there is always a lot of post;
2) there are always a lot of elderly locals who have very little post who come in after me;
3) there is always only one out of a possible three cashier tills open;
4) every parcel I bring out of the post bag is a different size and weight, or has to go to, say, Northern Ireland, so each parcel has to be weighed and individually stamped;
5) all the parcels I post may look slightly suspicious to pensioners and mothers huffing and tutting in the growing queue behind me;
6) this takes absolutely ages.

Now I mentioned that the parcels look suspicious, and this is due to the clever packaging we use for the Fan Club packs and photos we send out. Normal envelopes are no good, and if you are sending out an A4-size magazine and a small video a normal paper envelope simply will not do. You can't use those padded jiffy envelopes either as they're just too expensive. So we use these special industrial plastic bag things, sometimes white and occasionally black. The black ones look even more suspicious and sexual as the plastic is an obvious close relation to PVC. These envelopes also have a strange porn-shop smell, which I find difficult to describe, but some readers will understand. These envelopes, or 'rhino' bags as they are known, are almost indestructible, and once they are done up are impossible to undo. This is the Fan Club's discreet packaging. It's perfect, it looks anonymous, doesn't tear open to reveal the boobs inside, but when I'm at the post office with piles of them and people stare I'm sure they know it's porn of some description that I'm shipping off.

So the post all goes out. 'Thank you' letters and repeat orders soon pour in, as do a few letters of complaint. Normally along the lines of: 'Dear Eve, I sent for your photos a month ago and they still have not arrived'. From the very start a small card system was put into place. Every new member has an index card. On this index card are all the member's details including his birth date, address, and also a list of the goodies he's ordered and the dates they were sent. When a complaint comes in we can see what's going on in an instant.

But after a while a noticeable amount of these 'Where are they?' letters started to come in. Only a few to start with but then a growing amount week by by week, until not only were photos going missing but also orders were disappearing before they even got to the Fan Club. Something was afoot. And when something like this is happening – it doesn't take you long to suspect someone at the Post Office.

I like postmen. Most of the ones I meet are jolly helpful. They work hard, they get up very early. I do not envy them but I occasionally envy their bicycles. Anyway, it was clear that someone along the line was taking a fancy to the mail coming in to the Fan Club PO Box. We'd all heard stories of Post Office lavatories being blocked up with birthday cards opened for the cash inside and flushed away, but to know it was going on with orders coming in to my sister was a little unsettling.

My sister spoke to the post office. She spoke to the local police. She took advice from David Sullivan, the porn mail order king of the world, and a solution was found. It was very simple. Every other day, we send ourselves orders. This sounds strange, but it works. We make up dummy envelopes to ourselves, use different handwriting, different envelopes, fill them with Fan Club leaflets, bits of card, anything that makes them look fat and inviting to your light-fingered postie. Occasionally we'd even stick two-pence pieces in there too, thereby adding to the overall attractiveness of the incoming mail. However, wrapped up in all this paper and card and money is a letter from the local police station on headed paper saying nothing more than 'YOU ARE BEING WATCHED'.

Eve or myself took these cunning little traps anywhere we were going and posted them back to the Fan Club. I'd be in London, I'd post a couple. Go to the seaside, post another couple, and so on. Send ten out a week and note how many came back alive. Within a couple of weeks the dummy post took effect and we were back to normal.

3

So it's all going very well. I work odd days for Eve and we both enjoy it. Her Fan Club is doing well, the post coming in is up and I see for the first time in my sister a desire to really succeed. She has drive, she is organised and puts me to shame. She has good ideas about how to please her fans, she knows instinctively what they want from her, and she knows exactly how to supply it.

She quickly develops a business head that I never knew existed anywhere in my family before. And so, with one successful Fan Club up and running she decides to make more hay while the sun shines brightly. And she expands. This is the mid-90s. Page 3 in the *Sun* is still extremely popular. All the topless models from the *Sport* are also hugely popular. Top-shelf mags are selling strongly. And so my sister approaches another top model, one by the name of Donna Ewin. Yes, Donna Ewin. I have no idea who the hell she is or even what she looks like until my sister shows me some of her photos. I get excited. Well, I can't help myself. This woman is absolutely beautiful. With massive knockers. And not just massive knockers but massive real knockers. In the glamour business she's known affectionately as Donna 'The Body' Ewin and she looks like a Greek goddess, albeit one from the East End of London.

When she isn't posing for topless shots she's a hard-working market trader on the Roman Road or somewhere like that and she's also learning 'The Knowledge'. Donna has never had any rude shots taken and she's never done hardcore. It's only big boobs and a bit of bottom that's on offer from Donna Ewin and nothing more. And certainly never any front bottom. If you ask me you don't need it. And what a great Page 3 name: Donna. Donna. It's sort of exotic and almost important, maybe even heavenly. Anyway, it's perfect for Page 3. Donna has also just landed herself the odd cameo role in *The Fast Show*. So she's a busy and extremely popular model at the moment.

The all-new business-minded Eve makes a deal with Donna and within a couple of months opens 'The Official Donna Ewin Fan Club'. Eve has posh new stationery organised for all Donna's Fan Club letters, she starts to advertise it and away the club goes. Eve is responsible for about 99% of the work, and Donna gets a good commission once a month. It suits everyone, and Donna has no financial outlay and very little inconvenience, she just has to supply new photos as and when, plus a little bit of gossip every couple of months for newsletters. My sister uses exactly the same methods, advertising strategy and mailing procedures as she had when she started her own club, and sure enough, after the first wave of advertising, fan mail for Donna begins to arrive. Sack loads of it. Great big sackloads of it. It's incredible, like all these men out there have been waiting desperately for this Fan Club to open. Surprisingly, though, the mail coming in for Donna still falls short of the rather staggering amount my sister receives. Surprising only because Donna has been a top glamour puss for years and my sister is relatively new to the business. Nevertheless the piles for both girls are more than impressive.

With two clubs on the go, and with more than half as much mail coming in on top of the usual, my responsibilities at the Fan Clubs now change. There are more envelopes to write out by hand. More packs to assemble. More post to get stamped. More index cards to make, track and file. And very occasionally I have to muck in and help to open the fresh mail coming in. So, for the very first time, I get to see some of this fan mail first hand. Most of it is normal – and often very sweet and organised, notes to say 'I love you' and 'Please can I join your Fan Club please.' But once in a while something a little different comes in. Child-like writing, confused spelling, really dirty paper, that kind of thing. To me this kind of letter is most unusual but to my sister this is totally normal. I'd been unaware so far of the vast range of correspondence my sister was being sent every day. I ask her about it now I have some kind of first-hand knowledge, and she reveals that since she started quite literally anything and everything has been sent to her. This obviously includes letters and cards, but also Eve gets sent used bus tickets, train timetables, restaurant menus, bizarre and useless ephemera from all over the place. Weird and confused tokens of love. And lots of photos of fans with their families. I really have no idea how much stranger it's all going to get.

Both clubs gain momentum. My workload continues to increase. And I'm beginning to work one day every week instead of once a fortnight. As usual I have countless new Donna membership packs to assemble, and these are lovely and simple. I take a pile of

9

glossy magazines. You may notice the use of the word 'glossy' here again. This is a very important word in the world of fan clubs and sex. If you just say 'magazine' or 'photo' it all sounds a bit normal. But if you say 'glossy magazine', and 'glossy photos', they immediately sound so much sexier, and maybe even a little ruder. Go on, say it, 'GLOSSY'. Say it slower. It's almost onomatopoeic. Anyway, I take a pile of glossy men's magazines, normally *Playbirds* or something like that. I open up the first page (resisting the urge to look further), and place inside it a large 10" x 8" glossy signed photo of Donna in a striking Page 3 style pose. On top of this, I place a set of 6" x 4" glossy snapshots of Donna 'on holiday' in various states of undress. And then on top of these I place Donna's standard Fan Club welcoming letter and also her newsletter explaining all about the latest shoots Donna has been working on, news of her taxi-driving exploits and a list of all the new sexy Donna shots that are now available exclusively to Fan Club members. Each new membership pack is then placed into a rhino bag, I make sure all the addresses are correct, the rhinos are sealed, the index cards created and updated, then it's down to Grannyville to catch the last post. Dead easy. Mundane, but in my situation mundane is good. It gives me time to think about what I may or may not do in the future, what career I might pursue in the years ahead. Or, and more importantly, what fresh second-hand madness may be lurking in the charity shop down the road.

   The little grumbly local post office is all now getting a bit much. It's a cute little place full of gossip and old wood, but it really is not efficient enough to handle the constant piles of plastic parcels we bring. So Big Sis decides to change the way things are done. She decides that we should head for home instead, and take our thumping great stash of filth to the post office at the end of the road we grew up in. We are in a place called West End, in one of the four dying corners of Aldershot. The post office sits next to a Working Men's Club that is all but shut down now, where the Beatles played once when no one knew who they were. This post office is run by a lovely man from Pakistan by the name of Mr Patel. It's a funny place, a converted corner house, all double-glazing on the outside and woodchip on the inside. As well as the more usual stuff such as envelopes and glue, here at Mr Patel's you can buy light bulbs, rubbish kiddy toys and a large selection of Happy Shopper cuisine. Mr Patel is a tall gentleman. He has large thumbs, perfectly evolved for pressing stamps quickly onto envelopes. He also has beautiful handwriting which I am envious of. His eyes light up when we draw up outside his shop and empty the boot of post. Within a few visits to Mr Patel's post office he tells us just to leave it all with him, he'll look after it, weigh it and stamp it all in his own time in the evening. This suits us all very well.

Dear Donna you are my Number one, FAN I
would like to Take you out on a date Be
cuse I think you are a Nice Looking Model
and a Nice Looking young woman My one
Dream is to take a page3 girl out on a date
I have Been Bying The Daily Sport for a
long Time Now Please Dont Think I am a
Pervert Becuse I am Not I Will Allso take
you to see The Shawshank Redemption if
it was on down My CiNema But it IS iNT
This lETTer is JUST for you

So what I am going to do is Rent it on video
Just for you

Darling Donna you are My Number one FAN
and AllWAYs Will Be for EVer and EVer
With All My loVe from ▉

XX X XX XXXXX
XXX XX XXXXX

Above and overleaf: The letter that sparks my interest in dirty fan mail. I'd never seen anything quite like it
before. I start to collect.

11

With All My love AgAin from ▮
I will Allso Toure you HORSE RIDING
As Well and to See Barry White
The one Model I Would like to take
out is you I Allso CANt drive a car
So I doNT No how to get to The Model
PArties with All MY love AGAiN from ▮
I Said MY DReam is to go out with a page
3 girl and That p..i. person is you and
you are Allso MY Favourite page 3 girl
With All My love AgAin from ▮
XXX
XXX
XXX

4

THE FAN CLUBS are selling love. Well, sort of. Topless photos really, but some see this as love. And so for the annual day of big love that is Valentine's Day, Eve pulls out all the stops for the adoring fans she is now serving so well. She designs and then orders thousands of personal Valentine's cards, with special Donna and Eve signatures and love messages inside. They are super, very pink and terribly sweet. Inside the card we place a list of sexy new private photos that can be bought at bargain special Valentine prices. We also include a newsletter with updates and Fan Club news. This news predominantly tells of where my sister and Donna have been over the last few months and where they will be headed in the near future. A few days before we are due to post our big parcels of love, Eve and I sit down in her front room. We sit amongst piles upon piles of unfolded cards, letters, envelopes and address stickers, and set about the mighty folding and assembling task.

While we are folding and assembling we watch the legendary film *Come Play With Me*. This 1976 sex film became a phenomenon because it ran longer in London than any other film ever, or so the story goes. I clearly remember, as a child, gazing up at the posters outside the Aldershot flea pit cinema and knowing something naughty was going on behind the late-night doors. The film was made by David Sullivan, he of Birmingham City Football Club and Sport Newspapers fame. I had recently become aware that David had become rather a close friend of my sister's. The star of the film, Mary Millington, and the young David Sullivan were an item in the 70s. David turned her into the British sex icon of that era. Before that she was a veterinary nurse. I can see he's maybe starting the same process now with my sister. He's certainly helping her career through his newspaper.

Anyway, the film stars Mary Millington, Alfie Bass and some of the Hill's Angels, those busty blonde babes from the old Benny Hill shows. In the film Mary wears amazing sunglasses. The acting is ever so slightly atrocious, which is exactly what you'd expect from a British sex comedy. The plot, such as it is, centres around the exploits of two forgers who somehow end up on a health farm that somehow turns into a health farm of sex. Sadly there is little or no sex to speak of. It's like *Carry On* only with more boobs, swear words and bum jokes, but it's not as good. It has quite dreadful music as well. And even a bizarre musical dance routine with all the birds twirling around in short nurses' outfits. The film was directed by George Harrison Marks, one of the legendary directors of British soft porn. George was also responsible for making the UK's first nudie film. In *Come Play With Me*, Harrison Marks not only directs but also stars as one of the foolish forgers. He wears a comedy wig and comedy teeth and looks utterly ridiculous.

But it's all endearingly British and old-fashioned. It obviously worked its magic back in its day and is a pleasant enough period distraction whilst bending card and licking envelopes. We then watch another video, that one where Demi Moore sleeps with Robert Redford for a million dollars. Rubbish. I go out for sweeties and buns.

As usual with these kinds of jobs, we finish the folding and stuffing work in the nick of time only by working well into the night. The piles of our very pink mail have to make it to the post office four days before Valentine's Day. We send everything second class, you see. To save Mr Patel's thumbs my sister has bought enough second-class stamps for the whole lot, but I foolishly tell her that the glue on stamps is fattening and so end up stamping thousands of envelopes all by myself. We leave the house with sacks of stamped, bulging pink mail and head to the main sorting office at Aldershot; no post box is big enough for the thousands of envelopes we have, and delivery to the main sorting office guarantees the love letters go the same night. All the postmen at the Aldershot depot know who Eve is. They know what she does. She signs pictures. She chats with them and laughs. It keeps them all sweet. They love it when she turns up. They look after her post.

The day after Valentine's Day, when the cards have arrived, been opened, read and worked their sex magic, the mail starts pouring back to us with new orders for new bargain photos and hundreds upon hundreds of 'thank you' notes. More work for all. It's obvious now that the business is going places.

Below: Bombarded with love and badly drawn hearts. Valentine greetings and well wishes flood in.

Hi I am Just writing to say all the best and lots of Love

5

THE WORKLOAD KEEPS on increasing. More new members join all the time. More and more orders pour in. My sister is busy on shoots, modelling and also spending time looking for a new home to live in. I'm busy trying to work out my own life. The Fan Club work is only part time and that's the way Eve likes it. It's the way I like it too. It gives me time to look for a smashing new career. Another part-time job comes out of a walk to my barber's. Three shops down from the barber's is a new shop. In the window is a large Victorian glass box. In the glass box is a small pig. It has two heads, eight legs and one body. On the top of the box is an old fairground sign and handbill announcing the arrival of 'The Chesham Beast'. It's a Victorian fairground sideshow freak. Groovy. Scary. Next to 'The Chesham Beast' is a handwritten notice stating that part-time help is required. I march in. After a brief chat the bearded owner, a man called Tony Dixon, offers me work starting the same week. I can juggle the Fan Clubs with a bit of work with antiques.

I tell my sister the news of this extra part-time work and she is pleased for me. Our father, who's dead now, used to be an antique dealer. As we were growing up our weekends were full of cramped early-morning journeys to antique fairs that appeared to be populated almost entirely by old ladies. Imagine, a family of five (I have a younger sister too), plus a huge assortment of antiques, all crammed into a Mini Clubman Estate. People must have wondered.

The good news is that this new antiques work won't interfere with the Fan Club schedules as it's only one day a week (if that) to start with. So work continues in the same pattern. I normally work on a Monday for or with Eve, and this way it gets the Fan Club work out of the way and then we have the rest of the week to do other things.

It suits us both. But Eve is eager to expand her Fan Clubs even more. The simple Fan Club formula and business systems she has put into place work well for her, have transferred perfectly to the new Donna club, and so our Eve now wants to apply it to other soft porn stars. And there are lots of them. Based on an important survey carried out by the *Sunday Sport*, Eve and Donna are the most popular models in all the land. Coming in a close third is Vida Garman, fourth is Shanine Linton, and riding high at number five is Louise Hodges. Again, I've never heard of these lovely ladies until my sister decides to sign them up. The deals are the same, my sister is responsible for sorting everything out, and the girls get royalties every month. Dead easy. Everyone is happy. However, the workload increases dramatically. We desperately need another pair of hands, despite the fact that this is the middle of the year, a slow time in the Fan Club calendar. Trouble with porn is that you can't really advertise for staff. Well, not in the local paper, shop or job centre. You can imagine it now, the advert in the newsagent:

Extra Hands Needed: Local Porn Business Expanding.

You can see how these things can be so easily misconstrued …

To make matters worse, Eve had recently employed a temp to do some databasing on the all-new Fan Club computer and she'd left at lunchtime when she found out it was filthy disgusting dirty porn she was working on. The upshot of all this is that Eve still needs a part-timer for one or possibly two days a week during the busier periods. And, yes, it is a porn business, so there are pictures of naked ladies that need putting into envelopes, a plentiful range of top-shelf magazines to pack into rhino bags. And, worst of all, now that the Official Vida Garman Fan Club is also open there are panties everywhere. Well, not everywhere, but there is a large box of silky red ones in the office corner. So this is not a job for the faint-hearted. It's also not a job for anyone who fancies a good old gossip out of work. It's quite a private little business, as are most porn-based companies. And on top of unshockable and discreet, we also need someone trustworthy, as there are postal orders and cheques coming in through the post every day. It's not going to be an easy position to fill. So, what do we do? Who can we find? In this, our hour of need, my sister turns to … our mother.

Our mother is a pensioner. I'd call her a posh pensioner. Well, she's conservative and she talks proper. My mother is also a widow. Men and sex do not interest her. She is into gardening, cats, gossip, biographies and long walks in the countryside with the special hiking socks I bought her at Christmas. She is a lifelong member of the National Trust. My mother is a clean-living woman, and one who never swears. I've heard her say 'bugger' once at dinner when a scoop of Cornish flipped out of the tub and splatted

17

on the floor, but apart from that I have never, ever heard her say a rude word. I also doubt she's had that many rude thoughts. She's not like that at all. And if she is then she's extremely good at hiding it. But remember she is a pensioner, and like many pensioners continually worries about money. Not because she hasn't got any, but because she likes spending. She likes wearing expensive second-hand clothes and keeping up the posh appearance. This all costs more than her pension can possibly bear, so I think the idea of mucking in with her daughter's growing business for a bit extra was too much to resist. And it wasn't going to interfere with her National Trust voluntary work. So my mother now joins the little part-time porno workforce. Good for her, I think. And with three members of staff, it's time for Eve to really push on with the three new Fan Clubs she has just opened.

Vida Garman (Fan Club No. 3)

SO, ALLOW ME to introduce the all-new Fan Club girls. First up, it's Vida Garman. Vida's not a word or name I am familiar with. I also have no idea what a Garman is. This delightful porn star has been in the business a long time. A long, long time. She started modelling topless for newspapers in the early 1970s. She now has a very 1980s look to her which I think is all down to her 1990s hairdo. She's got a classic 'pin-up' look. She's very pouty, extremely sexy in some shots (when her hair is good) and has eyes that not only say 'Come to bed, you naughty boy' but also say 'Come to bed and let's be very dirty and while we're there I can teach you several tricks the like of which you have never even dreamed of or read about anywhere in your life.' Well, that's my opinion. Her photos are racy, rude and suggestive. There's a lot of bending over going on. There's also a lot of classic glamour-style posing, a twist in the body that allows both boobs and bum to be revealed to the lucky onlooker at the same time. Sometimes, and as mentioned, her weird hairstyles can let all this excellent posing down a bit, but most fans are not interested in the hair on her head so it makes no difference. Because of her enormous experience in the business I see Vida as the great-grandmother of British soft porn. She is tireless, works all the time, is guaranteed to please and also has a couple of lovely kids.

Shanine Linton (Fan Club No. 4)

RIGHT, SHANINE. Another name I am blissfully unaware of. I have never heard of a Shanine before. But what a little minx. And what a very experienced young woman. She's been in the business a good few years, since she was seventeen I think, and yet still manages to look seventeen now with the right make-up and outfit. Both slim and sexy, Shanine is great at playing the naughty teenager, the sex-mad schoolgirl, the little angel who likes to sin, she thrives upon these naughty porn personas. Shanine has real tits and a great arse. Most of the photos we have of Shanine are of her great arse. The Arse of Shanine is so popular it's now got a personality all of its own. It's all curvy and biteable, accessible and inviting. This is very good for the fans. Shanine is also a singer, songwriter and piano player. She has been writing her first album for about three years. Or is it four? I can never remember. Shanine is also very bubbly. Good fun. Sweet and a bit naughty. I like Shanine.

Louise Hodges (Fan Club No. 5)

LOUISE HODGES IS the kinky end of British soft porn. She's good old-fashioned naughty fun, ruder than most soft-porn stars, and Louise loves to wear all the kinky outfits she can get her busy hands on. Most of the shots we have of Louise are of a kinky nature, but of a very soft kinky nature. There's Louise in one of those black domination-style hats. There's Louise holding up a whip. There's Louise bending over holding the whip and wearing thigh-length rubber boots. There's also Louise topless in full rubbery bondage gear. Louise is very chatty and loves the business. If anyone was ever going to be a porn star it is Louise Hodges. She turns up on time, she rings to see if she can help, constantly works on shoots here and abroad. Louise sometimes gets odd jobs on the telly as a stripper, normally in detective-style shows. As a result she wants to work for telly as a professional make-up and hair artiste. Because Louise is a little kinkier and ruder than the other girls, her official Fan Club is adorned with an 'X'. It's the Official Louise Hodges X-Rated Fan Club. This, to most of the punters, promises an extra level of rudeness. It says that this club is definitely for adults only, so you'd better be 18-plus if you want to join.

It's important that I know all this background guff because from now on I have to write all the girls' newsletters on the brand new Fan Club computer. This is not a big job as there are only four or five newsletters a year per girl. And, as I used to be a copywriter in advertising, the process of writing these newsletters is simple. The process of researching these newsletters is, however, slightly more complicated. It starts by my phoning up each of the girls in turn (sadly, they don't all live together, lesbian-style, in one big soapy bubble-filled flat). I am then meant to have a little chat with each of them; asking them what they've been up to and what they've got coming up, etc.

However, it's never that simple because, in the main, the girls are never ever in and never ever return any calls. They have better things to do with their valuable time. So the research I have to make usually takes at least two weeks to sort out. The answers I do eventually get are rarely inspirational or newsworthy enough for the Fan Club members so I normally end up embellishing what little, if anything, the girls have told me. I write about the girls' holidays, recent photo shoots, their boyfriends (but only if they've just chucked them), their pets; the whole idea is to give their adoring fans a little picture of what is going on, to bring them a little closer to their girls. At the same time, the newsletters are 50% sales letters and the brief is to advertise as much new merchandise as possible in the limited A4 space I have. These newsletters go in every brand new Fan Club membership pack. And when these three new clubs start up, Eve makes sure that the new membership pack for each brand new girl is different from the packs we are already sending out for the other two clubs. She introduces subtle differences: all Vida Garman fans get photos, a magazine and a brand new pair of silky red ladies' panties. All Louise Fan Club packs are sent out with a mini guide to massage parlours with those rude phone numbers in the back. And Shanine fans get a huge amount of photographs of their idol in a vast array of different outfits.

The free pair of panties sent out to each new Vida member prove to be popular. Like, really popular. Too popular in fact. The new members write in for more. Within a few months of starting the all-new Vida club all the girls begin selling their undies in every new newsletter that is sent out. Each time we try to change the style of undies available, making them more exciting and more irresistible to our burgeoning gang of fans. We have the simple plain but silky ones. We have big ones. Some are teeny tiny. Some have gussets, some have not. Some are lacy, some are see-through. Some have rude writing on the front. Some have a naughty split up the back. Some have a large suggestive opening at the front.

This handsome array of lingerie needs a steady supplier, a good panty man. A reliable sort. To start with we get them all from some bloke my sister knows. All good quality, all well priced. And now as part of my job I have to be constantly on the look out for cheap female underwear. I discover that most street markets have cheap new undies for sale. Even cheaper in bulk. And to my surprise nearly every charity shop I enter I start to see old ladies' knickers. Not nice, obviously popular with the old dears, but not suitable for Fan Clubs. Pants turn up at boot fairs too. I've never really noticed before but ladies' knickers are everywhere. The best place for me and knickers, though, is the East End of London. Petticoat Lane and its surrounding streets. It is here I now begin to buy lots of groovy, sexy undies in bulk. I buy them, and the girls sell them to their eager fans. And it doesn't stop there. The fans want more and more. They want stockings. They demand bras. I go back to the East End and buy both in large quantities and in all different sizes and styles. There's a great shop I always go to, run by the masters of bulk underwear retail, the Bangladeshis. These guys really are the inherent masters of selling everything in vast quantities. They like doing deals. I turn up at the shop with cash. They offer me coffee. They show me truckloads of new and sexy undergarments. They are friendly, yet totally relentless. I never explain what I need the undies for. They keep asking. To all their questions I say nothing. They are curious, I deflect. They keep guessing, I avoid. Within a few weeks they call me The Bra Man. I am honoured.

It's here and now, with the five clubs really taking off, that my sister moves. Everything moves. The relationship with her man is getting more serious. She's been driving to Essex from deepest Surrey about three or four times a week to see him, and the situation is getting daft. She has to move closer to him. Mother still lives in Aldershot. Mr Patel's post office is in Aldershot. But the boyfriend is in Essex. So yet again my sister does the whole organised thing that she is so famous for, gets a map out and puts a big circle in the area exactly equidistant between Aldershot and Essex. Next, she drives to the circle on the map and buys a property. She moves like lightning and with military precision to Buckinghamshire. The properties are bought and sold in less than a week. We move all the office to her new larger home, a place that can only be described as a footballer's house. Modern, large, luxurious and totally private. With big, big gates that are really too big. And it's just down the road from Roger Moore. The all-new Fan Club office is installed in a large featureless room, the study area behind my sister's new grand kitchen. And once we're settled in, the filing cabinets moved, runs all the way back to Mr Patel's post office organised, and with a brand new second-hand plans chest bought to store sexy photos inside, Eve opens another Fan Club. It really is starting to get relentless.

Charmaine Sinclair (Fan Club No. 6)

CHARMAINE IS THE top black sex model in the UK. She looks amazing. She has a great face. She has an incredible body, very slightly enhanced by cosmetic surgery I believe. But it's very subtle so you'd never really know. Her smouldering sexy looks and beautiful black skin are perfect for the more exotic shoots and so most of the delightful and fairly sexy Charmaine photos we have are set on beaches, in lagoons and in hot, sweaty jungles. Super. And a great contrast to all the other Fan Club girls' merchandise. Charmaine is still young but has been in the business for quite a while. Charmaine dreams of leaving soft porn well behind her and becoming a serious writer. She is a determined young woman. Educated too. I'm sure she'll succeed. We couldn't think of a novelty for the Charmaine Sinclair Fan Club bumper membership pack, but it doesn't make much difference. Loads of men join almost the second it opens.

MEET THE GIRLS
– Part One –

Above, right and overleaf: Meet some of the girls Donna, Eve, Vida, Shanine, Louise and Charmaine.

Louise

Charmaine

6

SO, MY SISTER is now running her own very lucrative business and doing it very well. She seems to be a total natural. She now has six Fan Clubs under her belt, she has just moved from a flat into her very own large, comfortable house and has just got a new sexy car. She is also constantly busy with new shoots, accounting, redecorating, gardening, it's bloody endless. Oh, and she's just also given birth to her first child, David. He looks like a little Eskimo. On the other side of the family there's me, the newly appointed Uncle Jonny. I have two very small part-time jobs for one or two days a week (if that) and struggle to pay my rent. And it's ever-so-slightly starting to get to me. I sit there, in the square room behind my sister's vast kitchen, every Monday doing the same as I did last Monday. The only variation being that there's more work, so I have to do it all quicker. I get annoyed at myself. I should by now have my own good job, my own little home, my own life sorted out. I should at the very least be heading in that direction. But it isn't and I'm not. The problem is I still don't know what to do, or what I want to do. I consider a life in porn, but really see no suitable opportunities in a business that is totally controlled by very few, very powerful people who are all as thick as thieves. I could continue with the antiques, I do love it but I don't see how it would ever turn into something you could even loosely call a career.

So what can I do with my life? I've always had a passion, born of my parents' exceedingly poor record collection and an early unhealthy obsession with charity shops. I buy old records – vinyl LPs – but specifically old film and TV records. Since I can remember I have bought TV and film music. In London as a copywriter I'd spend my lunchtimes trawling through record stores and making extra dinner-money selling LPs bought from charity and boot fairs the weekend before.

Back home in London I find a forgotten old music archive. It's a little music library, called Bosworth & Co, in Soho, just off Regent Street. It's not like a book library, no, music libraries are very different. Bosworth & Co had produced old stock music for TV and film back in the 1950s and 1960s. Stock music is the kind of music they use for advertising and sitcoms, drama or sex films when there is no money to get other music composed. A good example of one of these Bosworth recordings was the fanfare played every time a guest entered the *This Is Your Life* studio – BA, BA-BA BAAAAAAAA. Another of these tracks was used to sell lavatory bleach in 1967. Like a fine wine this period muzak has matured wonderfully and now sounds superbly weird and strangely fresh. It's avant garde noise, it's spooky jazz. It's all dead groovy and no one has really heard any of it properly before. It's lost music. I knock on the door of their offices. I walk in and pass into some kind of surreal twilight zone. Everyone seems about 60, and slightly strange and wonky. The place is full of dust and piles of old droopy sheet music. The man at the front desk looks like a pensioner and a schoolboy at the same time. He shouts hello at me. I ask to see the head man. He points and shouts. I squeeze past more dusty piles into the head man's vintage office, introduce myself and ask very nicely if I can issue their wonderful lost music properly as a modern record. Word spreads around the few members of Bosworth & Co very quickly and excited murmurs begin. They all think I'm insane. So they say yes. A few weeks later and all my mates muck-in with effort and saved cash and together we issue this all-new and quite ridiculous LP on the all-new label we invent called Trunk Records. There is no great reason we call it Trunk Records, it just makes us laugh. Once we have paid for production of the record we have no money left to promote it. So instead we decide to do something a little sensational with it for the press. As we know, through my sister's business I have access to lots of pants. So we send out pairs of perfumed pants to record magazines with a little Trunk logo and the statement 'Found on a dark street in Soho'. The next day we send the same people the record with the same statement. It may well be contrived and confusing to most but there is a little truth in it all, and it works quickly in our favour. The press remember it. They listen. We then release the record and people in record shops start talking about it. And selling it. We get great reviews for the LP, people phone us up about it. It's all very jolly, exciting and surprising.

So I now have three part-time jobs. Porn, antiques, and records. Sooner or later I know I'm going to have to choose where to jump for the rest of my life, but the only way I can carry on is to work at them all part time and study them all like an apprentice. I may not have a proper career but I must be fantastic to sit next to at dinner parties.

7

MEANWHILE, BACK AT the Fan Club ranch, there is a hell of a lot of mail coming and going out for all these girls. Every day my mother or sister collects the mail from the PO Box (which is still in Aldershot), then sorts it into piles for the different girls, orders get separated from postal orders and cheques that come in, there's a pile for queries, cards and ephemera too. Once these piles are separated, the relevant ones are placed in the corresponding girl's file. I then go through these files and work out exactly what is needed for each girl's orders – how many sets of photos will be needed in total, how many pairs of panties, that kind of thing. This ensures we don't run out of anything and no fan is kept waiting too long for his goodies. Any missing orders I have to trace, any query I have to deal with. It's a little tedious but I know how to do it all. We all just get on with what we have to and I know that when it's over the rest of the week is free for antiques and weird 60s musak.

I'm sure you can imagine the amount of post that is now pouring in for all these girls, I mean there are six established sex Fan Clubs on the go, and they're all popular girls. There are sacks of the stuff coming in every week. And in amongst it all we begin to notice patterns of repetition starting to appear. Fans who write in every week, sometimes twice a week every week to just one girl – the monogamist. Or we have the polygamist who writes to all the girls on a very regular basis. These men I call serial writers. These are the men who write far, far more than normal and, by virtue of their prolific pens, become instantly recognisable, either by what they write or how they write. My sister is aware of them way before anyone else, because my sister never misses a trick. After a while and because Eve is often away, my mother supervises all the incoming mail and so she becomes aware of them too, although she seems to remark more on the content, because a high proportion of them write in a surprisingly unique and extremely filthy way. And of course I see all the mail now, so I notice them too.

Spunky Arthur

I'LL BEGIN WITH Spunky Arthur and the first thing to point out is that Spunky Arthur is Arthur's very own porn nickname. He signs off all his correspondence with the signature 'Spunky Arthur'. He is a pensioner from Croydon. He is in his mid 70s. His wife died a decade or more ago. He lives alone, but with a toy dog. He never names the dog in any of the letters. Spunky Arthur either hand writes his letters or types them immaculately on an old typewriter with a two-colour ribbon. He puts all his expletives in CAPITALS. He writes to five of the six girls on a regular basis. He buys everything from every newsletter they send, and then buys it all again a month later. He buys every photo and all the undies he is offered. My mother is always shocked by the explicit content of every Spunky Arthur letter. In fact if she opens one there is normally an embarrassed squeal followed by the simple phrase 'disgusting'.

```
      Love and Kisses
        your dirty old man
          and SPUNKY
              Arthur.
          ARTHUR.
    XXXXXXXXXXXXXXXXXXXXXXXXXXXX
```

28.8   38.90 + £20 p.o

Hello Darling.
        Arthur here, please find £20 P.O. for your fan
Club membership and Cheque for £38.90 for an order also
order form.
        What pictures I have seen of you your TITS look
brilliant. My other Fans are Eve, Shanine, Louise, and Vida
and now I am joining your Club, so I now have five Sweet-
hearts, all lovable and Fuckable.
        Just a short letter with my Order and form
including fan club Payments.
        Hope to hear from you soon Sweetheart.

                    All my Sexy LOVE and KISSES
                    from your SPUNKY

                              Arthur.

                        ARTHUR.
        XXXXXXXXXXXXXXXXXXXXXXXXX

32

Arthur types, Arthur writes. Note the ticks on both letters – this means the letters have been dealt with.
Figures at the top are Fan Club codes.

28. 3

33

Darling Spunky Louise.

Come to my arms you beautiful charms. Just squeeze your Tits against my body and your Cunt. I will squeeze your Bum and give it a gentle slap, I am already for you my Prick is semi-stiff you would take him in your mouth and work him big, hard and thick while I lick your Cunt and Bum-hole then I would Fuck your Bum-hole, and your big Tits, and your Spunky Cunt all the way.

You are so lovable, Fuckable you give a lovely Fuck. Hold on I am just about to unload my Spunk I cant hold it any longer, you are Spunking as well you naughty girl, I love you when you are naughty, rude and talk dirty.

Darling Spunky Shanine.

　　　　Many thanks for the Calender and Video's which I enjoyed very much indeed you naughty girl, but I love every minute of it. I was lying down just in my Stockings, Suspenders,Bra with my 38" TITS and Knickers I just SPUNKED in my Knickers I couldn't hold it any longer.

　　　　You and I are going to be very naughty which I am going to tell you about which will make you SPUNK when you read this letter and I hope you don't throw it away when you have read it?

　　　　My long, thick, hot, throbbing PRICK and myself are fine thank you. I am in the right mood for being naughty and filthy, so be prepared for what I write.

　　　　All you five SPUNKY, SEXY Beauties get me hard and SPUNKING on a regular basis, Eve,Louise,Vida,Charmaine, and yourself. It is a shame you can't send me your CUNT so I can FUCK it all the time, and I wish I could send you my long, thick, hot, SPUNKY, throbbing PRICK so you can put it in your SPUNKY CUNT and have a good FUCK.

　　　　Now I will tell you what I would do to you. First I would cuddle and a big hug and give you a nice big FRENCH KISS, then I would slowly undress you till you were only inyour your Stockings, Suspenders, and Knickers and leaving your fantastic TITS bare and would give you another FRENCH KISS at the same time I would fondle and caress your TITS and NIPPLESand and you would play with my hot PRICK and hairy BOLLOCKS and I would then finger-FUCK your hairy CUNT by this time I would have SPUNKED in your hand and you would lick all the SPUNK off your hand and swallow it.

　　　　I would then take you to the toilet and you would hold my PRICK while I have a PISS at the same time I would finger-FUCK you again, then you would have a PISS at the same time I would put my long,thick, hot, SPUNKY, PRICKin in your mouth and play with you TITS, then would take you into the Bedroom and you would lie on your backwith with your legs up on my shoulders and I would slide my SPUNKY PRICK deep into your CUNT and you would grip it tight with your CUNT muscles and you would make me unload all my SPUNK into your CUNT until you sucked me dry.

　　　　Before I forget I received the SEXY order on the 17-10-96.
I would put my finger up your Bum-hole, also I would put my throbbing PRICK in between yo your TITS and unload my thick, white, creamy SPUNK on your TITS and you and I would rub it all in, then I would put my PRICK in your mouth and empty all my SPUNK till I was dry Sweetheart. I am sure you will be all wet and SPUNKING when you read this letter won't you? I LOVE YOU DARLING.
　　　　　　All my LOVE,SEX, and KISSES
　　　　　　　　from your SPUNKY
　　　　　　　　　　Arthur.
　　　　　　　ARTHUR.
　　　　　XXXXXXXXXXXXXXXXXXXXXXXX

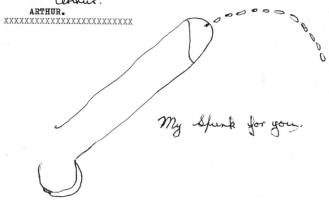

My Spunk for you.

Hello Darling.
    Many thanks for the Newsletter and Order Form which I
am returning with a Cheque for £62-50. I received letter on
the 16-9-96.
    I will come and keep you warm, I would even like to
send you my long thick Prick to you wrapped in cotton wool
so when you go to bed you canpush it up your thick hairy
Cunt. I am writing this letter to you in my Stockings,
Suspenders, Knickers, and my 38" Tits which I walk about the
house in, it is a fantastic feeling.
    You have a fantastic pair of Tits, I would like tò get
my long, thick Prick in between those lovely TITS and give th
a severe Fucking.
    You will be getting a lot more naughty, Sexy letters
in the future, I am going to love you.
        All my LOVE and KISSES
        from your SPUNKY

        ARTHUR.
    XXXXXXXXXXXXXXXXXXXXXXXXX

Geoffrey

SAY HELLO TO Geoffrey. He writes once in a while to my sister but mainly corresponds with Charmaine Sinclair. Most of his letters follow the same simple pattern. For a start they arrive just about every week. They look identical, always on the same small blue-lined writing paper. And always blue biro. Geoffrey has neat, organised writing. However, he seems far too excited when writing to use any punctuation at all. His letters are nearly always about his dreams. These dreams are extremely frequent. On a good week there will be two dreams and therefore two corresponding visits to the post box. Some of Geoffrey's dreams are longer than others, running sometimes to three pages, but normally he averages a single yet very full page.

Before we go any further it's important to point out that many of Geoffrey's letters (and there are many) end with his 'Big Rising Willie'. We all understand this simple statement. However, just to hammer home the image, Geoffrey sends in, on a regular basis, images of his upwardly mobile best friend.

1) These photos always arrive ready framed to ease placement onto your desk or bedside table.

2) The offending member always points in the same downward direction, which I find vaguely odd.

3) These delightful, life-sized gifts, including the plastic gold frame, measure no more than 1 inch by half an inch. It may be 'rising', it can certainly be described as a 'willy', but, as each framed portrait so cruelly reinforces, it most certainly isn't 'big' Geoffrey.

And yet, for reasons unknown to myself, I have one of these particular framed icons perched upon the top of my monitor in the office.

6.6. Sent
Turkish delight

Dear Sexy Charmaine
You are very Beautiful
sexy Woman and you are
Gorgeous and you Really Turned
me on wild, Really wild and I
would Like To spend the Evening
with you In my Local Pub or Restaurant
and Because I Love Going out a
Date with you To Going see the
show or the Cinema and the Pub
and Fish & chip and Going To the
Hotel and sex with you.
Love From ██████

Dear Sexy Charmaine
        I Have a Dirty Dream
About you and your Friend Sam
Jessop and the Both Touched the
Body Together and your Friend
Touched your Sexy Body and
the Both Togched Sexy Boob and
rising Nipple and the Both Togched
Sexy Pussy and the Both Togched
Sexy Bum and the Both Togched
Sexy Leg and your Friend But
your Lips on you and you But
your Lips on your Friend and
I wake up my Big Rising Willie
                    yours Sincerely

10.9.48.55   Page 1

Dear Sexy Charmaine

Every Night I Go To Bed I
Looked at you on The photo and your
Eye is looked at me and you
Really Turned me on Wild, Really
Wild and I Have a Dirty Dream
About you and I But my lips on
You and you But your Lips on Me
and We Both Kiss Together and
I But my Hand on your Big Boob
and I Touched your Big Boob and
I Touched your Rising Nipple and
I suck your Rising Nipple and I
But my Hand on your Pussy and

I Touched your pussy and I lick
your pussy and I But my Hand
on Your Sexy Leg and I Touched
your Sexy Leg and I lick your
Sexy Leg and I But my Hand
on your sexy Bum and I lick
your Sexy Bum and I Fuck
you and you Fuck me and we
Fuck All Night and we Fuck All
Day and We Both Fuck Together
and my Radio Alarm when off
and I wake up and that was My
Real Dream and my Big Rising
willie was very Hardest Rock
and you But your Hand on My
Big Rising willie and you Touched
my Big Rising willie and you suck
my Big Rising willie and You But
your Hand on my Leg and you

Touched my Leg and you But
your Hand on my Bum and
you Touched my Bum and.
you Lick my Bum and you
But my Big Rising Willie on
your pussy and In The Hole and
I Fuck you and you Fuck me
and we Fuck All Night and we
Fuck All Day and we Both Fuck
Together and we Fuck, we Fuck
we Fuck, and I wake up and that
was my Dream and my Biggest
Rising Willie was very Hardest
rock.
            Love From ███████

My Messages
    I Fuck you and you Fuck me
and we Fuck All Night and we fuck
All Day and we Both Fuck
Together and we Fuck.

Anthony

I BELIEVE ANTHONY to be a lonely man. I believe it because he admits to it regularly, and I have no reason to doubt him. For me Anthony really sums up the whole point of pornography, and it's something I'd never really thought of until I began getting involved in the business. It's a service industry. Modern journalism frequently tells us that a little porn in a relationship can spice it all up a bit, and that's all well and good, but I believe this type of use contributes only a minuscule part of the porn business revenue. I think porn is far more about men like Anthony. Anthony spends a lot of time alone. He is a man, flesh and blood, and he instinctively needs and desires a female but has absolutely no idea how to get one. Why this has happened I really have no idea. There could be any number of explanations. What I do know is that he writes to Shanine and Eve all the time asking for help and advice. It's best if you just look at Anthony's letters and work it out for yourself. For me this is all terribly sad. When I see Anthony's letters I realise just how lucky I am.

Darling
SHANINE LINTON
████████ IS a LONELY
MAN. WOH is seeking
a young WOMAN WOH,
LiK MAN WITh hair on
The fACe

1.8.20

darling SHANINE
LINTON

I want too
ENLARGE MY COCK
BY 4 INCHES. MY
COCK IS only 5
8 INCHES

P.S. The REASON
I want a Big COCK
for so yoy can
Suck MY Big penis

/MY SPECIAL MESSAGE\

penis /

My Special Message Penis – a memorable sign-off

30.8. No money

Darling SHanine LINTON

I am FeDyp with.
My Self because I youly
Wank a LoT. BuT
I GoT feDyp with Sex.

I Looking aT You. Do

you Think I Shoild STop

Looking aT The pHoto's

of you, please WRiT Back
to my Bout This PRoBLom

darling SHANINE
THANK You for The pHoTo's.
You SeND ME TherevVery
Sexy, please Could I SeND
a pHoto of My Cock,
  please WRiTe Back too Lit
ME KNow. if I GAN SeND a
pHoto of My cock or pénis,

This is The size of
My cock 5 inch

Penis →

Penis

44

Darling
Here a PHOTO OF ME DO
you Think I HAM to ugly too

have sex with. TELL ME The
~~Tru~~ Tur please

Personla message
P$ would you Like too

PLAY with my Penis

My personal message is

Wahtc my penis off
SHANINE LINTON

_____

Prick

Willy

Cock

Dick

Penis

Trevor

TREVOR IS AN unusual fan. For a start, he is not a member of any Fan Club, but this minor point never stops him writing in on a regular basis. I normally have to deal with Trevor as the girls are not interested in him at all. He sends no money, and is just one of hundreds of begging writers we get every month. But Trevor is different from most of the other beggars, purely because he absolutely refuses to give up in his quest for free filth. Every time he writes I send him the standard membership application forms which he never returns. Instead, Trevor writes back using his own cunning mixture of undying devotion and outright pleading that gets him absolutely nowhere. I admire his efforts. What I find odd is that he occasionally, and quite possibly out of sheer desperation, requests free pictures of the girls with their clothes on, which simply do not exist.

46

MY HEART

Yours
forever!!

428

8.2. NO money

Do you answer this?

6'

Dear Vida,

just a note. Hope your keeping well! I have a love for you as a friend! and think of you So! do You know you have My loyalty for life? I have Very Strong feelings for You, like a brother!! I'm going to be here for you always You give Me hope in the way My life's going!!

I'm not going to give up on you. Many Men think of you just for sex but for Me your far More Mean that!! You are More a real Woman to Me than Anything! Thank You!! I hope you will always be happy! and you will always have friends! You Mean a lot to Me!

Dear Vida,

I pray this year has started as intended? family is well and you are fine? I can't stop thinking of you, May be its because i care! I'm not going to give up on you, My friendship is to strong.

I write this between Renal appointments! My health these days is not so good, but My heart is strong with a love for you!

I would like to be a personal friend forever if you will let me? So much more than a fan and not as those you work with! I don't want a phyiscal relationship with you, You mean so much more than that! nothing else but true friendship!!

A woman i can trust to be a round to talk to and honour and share with!! Think of me like a brother!! a safe place to unload your worry's a male heart who cares! a soft kiss to say i'm here for you! a stroke of your hair to show i'll stand by you always!

███████

×××

Ps. want to buy lots of clothed photos of you signed Don't need to see you naked to show i care!

×××х

5.9.En-q

My HEART
Yours
forever!!

Dear Miss. Hodges,

        I know you will find this
letter Strange! at a time when we are saddened
by the death of Diana Princess of Wales. I felt a deep
need to write to you! Dear Miss Hodges you are
such a very beautiful lady. I feel the same way
about you as many of the world thought about
our Princess, but more so, because I'm able
to say so much with truth to you in this
letter. I CARE ABOUT YOU! I LOVE YOU!! "Not in
a Sexual way as you might think!" I feel for you
care, love you as a person not just as many do.
as a sex object. I know you must have many friends
and people that care about you? I know also
many men write to you to join your fan
club. if I had that kind of money I would
my self join just to show you I care. SORRY!!

    all I ask in this letter is to be able.
to call you a persnal friend! I will always be here for
you as such. you can write me always. you are in
my thoughts and my Prayers. I would also be honowed
if I could have a signed photo of yowself as I
would tresure it always.   P, T.O.

48

At the end of the day all I wanted
to say is " I give you my self in
friendship and would be honoured
to call you friend!! please take care in
all you do at and know you will never be
a lone because I'll be always here for you.
   Take care my precious friend!

              Love, and Bless you
                 always ▆▆▆▆
                                    x x x

P.S. I'm sorry if my
    letter upsets you
 I felt I had to write
  to tell you how I feel!
                 sorry!
                    xxxx

P.P.S
   STAY HAPPY iN ALL you

Do!!
      I'll honour
           you always
              ∧

              x   x   x

Stanley

THIS IS STANLEY. An ex-military type. Stanley is a bottom man. His favourite bottoms are those belonging to Shanine and Louise. It only takes the right shot from the right angle of just one of these pert posteriors to ignite Stanley's interest, an interest that is then extremely hard to extinguish. Stanley also has his own bottom-based belief system. These beliefs are based on the ancient Egyptian sexual mythologies that explain 'The Secret Centres'. These Centres are all over the body but the most important and most Secret Centre of all is in the bottom area. Stanley is writing a book about this right now, so all will become clear when it's published. Stanley, as you will observe, always writes in haste. To catch the post. Nevertheless this need for speed does not stop him writing letters of extraordinary length, 12–16 pages is the norm for Stanley. There's a certain elegance in the stream of botty-obsessed consciousness that is the Stanley letter, all wonderfully embellished with the most spectacular punctuation.

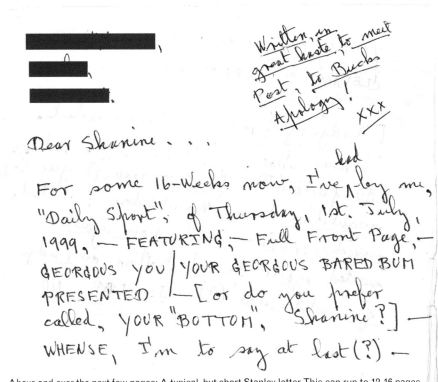

Above and over the next few pages: A typical, but short Stanley letter. This can run to 12-16 pages, often with large addendums.

— Well (!) — never in all my life before. — [See that either in some Mag.; or, "in the flesh", some Girl-friend's, Lady-friend's, bared bum past] — have I seen "female-bared-full-bottom", Darling, [that, even begins approach the .HEAVENLY EROTIA OF YOUR'S/ OF YOUR WONDROUS BUM-CLEVAGE BETWEEN . . .

[Judgeing from the "tennis rackets", "tennis shoes", "tennis hat" set in the photo (?) — the Scenario, [I guess!;), would've been "Wimbledon"? — But, whichever (?) — Just how you're "seated" your bared bottom over edge of "white stool" (?) — IS FAB, NO LESS. . .

3

Obviously — [as evidence by your
Bared Bum Presented; and, what I've
said in admiration of you there...]—
—[doubtless...]— We're (BOTH) very
much, "female-bum-conscious/aware..."

Looking, at YOUR'S, Darling, in the
pic. (?) I'm sure, sure absolutely,
that you've been [ever] aware of
your own loveliness there; and,
this, yes, going-back to "tenderest
years", as early as Age 5,(!) at
least... "Female Bottom"— [as
YOUR'S, Shanine...]— isn't Erotica
that, subsequently, (somehow) "appears":
No! — Your were blest of this, by
"Mother Nature",[in the first place]; and,
at once, by The Mother-Giving Shanine

Birth, [in the second place]. 4

[WHENSE, perhaps, "The Lady" would
appreciate. you telling her, I'd said
so !!! [at some convenient
early opportunity...?]

I would dare ask you now, what
I haven't dared ask before, viz-

To-spell-it-out...? — Do you
have, Naked Photoset available? —
OF YOU / OF YOUR BARED BUM / OF YOUR
BARED BUM-CLEVAGE, [PRESENTED...]
as explicitly, as you (alone) know
your bared bum can "show"?

This Photo, in "Daily Sport",
— SUGGESTS — Shanine. would've known

"getting", her bottom bared   5
and spanked, as a Teenager,
"parentally", at home. . . .

The "Daily Sport", presents you,
"having-very-smackable-female-full-
-bum. (. . .)

If any Photoset is to hand(?) I'd
dearly love shots, OF YOU/OF YOUR
BARED BOTTOM, as in the "Daily Sport"
pic. — but, with-you-bending-
right-over-the-stool-[to-be-spanked];
rather, than, "sitting-on-it" . . . . O.K?

In advance of sending [any] such
Photoset (?) — Will you let me
know the cost? Whence, I will

6

dispatch cheque for the amount,
by Return Post . . .

In conclusion — [at risk of being
boring?] — [I say again . . .],
vis —

YOU, shanine, (have) most
gorgeous, sumptuous,
sensuous, Female Bared
Bum, KNOWN ANYTIME, or
ANYWHERE . . . [by me, anyway.]

And, YOU KNOW, — that's, — NO OVERSTATEMENT

I love you, there . . .

love,

▮▮▮▮▮

XXX

TO: P7

7

N.B.   As for, those " 3 - Kisses ",
(above given (?) — Please
receive [each], whereon (?),
as follows —

      a) On (your) Mouth-lips;

      b) On (your) Fanny-lips;

and,   c) On (your) [You-Know-What?]
[Most-Important-Of-
All . . .]   YES, —
sharing, ON "SECRET-
CENTRE", OF YOUR
BARED BOTTOM
PRESENTED . . .

XXX

> the greate full (still nutty)
> is you a signed photograth
> of Helle & she one The nicesit
> girls from SCANDINAVIA she
> could Let have Sex in any
> where possable in any
> POSITON & be satisfied for Life
> and Eve eib I coont the
> GIRLS signed photographs
> then I you be my princess
> & take you on a blow Job worth
> rebering & fuch you any way
> you Like it Starbery and cream
> I like it of with chocolate
> I take you goped with any time
> any place & GHOT Spots for
> Spore is now Love as ever
>
>   x x x   EVE
> keep watching this
> space for more sex
> please darling
>   x x

Daniel

THERE'S ONLY ONE Daniel. He writes to all the girls every week. In red or in blue ink. When a new Fan Club opens, Daniel is normally there in amongst the first few letters. It gets very hard, though, to work out exactly what Daniel is after. He sends in postal orders and never really explains what they're for. My sister decides that, after having first tried to write for an explanation, there is no point in getting too involved and she just sends him photos he hasn't already got. This seems to suit Daniel as he sends in an order every week without fail. It takes a little time to get your eye tuned into Daniel's fast, explosive handwriting, but once you're locked in, it can get wild. Daniel also has a thing about strawberries, cream and chocolate. He also mixes panto, TV and films with sex. Which is nice.

Dear Darlings
I to have a dirty pair panties worned
by My No1 Faverate girl
I like Take you all the way Easey Pink
Pussy I like like Sexsul Strawberry
and cream like Custard fights
Me and fingering each other in
40 TomaTo KeChup and slapping
your titties on top of Me & Ramming
your arse in My face I give My Coch
in your Mouth I do Route 66
Postion & doggy Seyle
Please get the New girls
Bonnie Simon Sara Jane Viki Thomas
to Sign My Calender Plus The adlele
and Teressa Mary and Sammy Jessop
and enjoy all My desires
from you I pedge My Soul
Sucking you in The Snow & Putice in
your BiKini you do & dirty blow Jobs
on The beach
I love to see ya Soon
you Take Me all way
So fuck Me you biTch
I am wanking you So I hope
you Perve are you wanking over
Me So I bet you My
Darling keep your Body
Moving over Me &
Keeping in the grove
to you darling
your Sincerly lover boy

Right now darling

I fuck you all out in the snow
TOTALY NUDE in a Igloo on top
of each other in strawberry and
chocolate + coffee and whipped
cream and custard and ice cubes
and plenty of water I lick your
ice cool pink Sunny Chunk
and go down in your cool golf holes
in the rear golf course and a hole in
one + spread EAGLE your lovely
arse and deeply rub your titties
in my face alet me swallow your
Juices all over me body let me take in
my mouth + give me a blowjob
to last a life time.
   before I go greetings
        from NORWAY
it goes like this Das raisen Den
Swollen Las Maisen ding FUCHTTEH
Da sa Las Always
   I suck you dirty anyway
you like it

P.S. My order is on the form

so be sexy dirty saucy
in reply
      love   lov
            LUV
         Hugs
      Cuddles Me fuck
                   Baby
  +xx   KISSES enjoy it
  King   xxx NORWAY
   of ENGLAND
        MOOSE EIK GRUNDIG

59

I am your sexo
FUCK me girl

DEAR ARE YOU FUCKING WELL NOW and POSTION you want for Ever cinderella on top I can caste sour wet Pink Pussy LIPS onto my cock will see like the shoe Ride all over sour bodies & I would be you DIRTY rotten prince charming I would Marry you VIRGIN STYLE

P.S. Put some pinkey lipstick on sandwich here to think of oy right in a bikini with smell the whip you would your Pussy cleopatra I would be cleopatra a roman slave in love with your lips you I hope you got my PRESENT on I love think of sex Plays dirty slow Jokes all over my body here to Ride you in a swimming Pool

P.S. Please put some sexies lipstick on the photograph for me so I can think in my dreams

Bryan

BRYAN LOVES ALL the girls, and as soon as a new Fan Club opens, Bryan is always the self-proclaimed NUMBER ONE FAN. Bryan writes very hard indeed. Look closely and you will see writing on one side coming through to the other. He really means what he writes. He must concentrate a lot. Bryan is a fully paid-up Fan Club member of all the Fan Clubs and therefore Bryan gets sent all the same newsletters as all the other fans on a regular basis but obviously does things with them at home. I don't know what exactly, he might throw them out for all I know, but he's endlessly writing in to demand them all again, and quickly too, because it's very urgent. He can never ever have enough newsletters. I'd say Bryan is possibly the most enthusiastic fan of all.

MARCH 17.2
DEAR LOUISE
THIS IS YOUR NUMBER
ONE FAN ▌▌▌▌▌ WRITING
TO YOU AGAIN PLEASE
CAN YOU SEND ME ALL
YOUR FULL SET OF ALL
OF YOUR FULL LISTS
PLEASE CAN YOU SEND
ME ALL YOUR FULL SET
OF ALL OF YOUR NEWS
LETTERS THAT YOU
P TO

2

HAVE SO I CAN SEE
EVERY THING THAT YOU
SELL FROM YOUR FAN
CLUB I WOULD LIKE TO
BUY A LOT OF THINGS
FROM YOUR FAN CLUB
PLEASE CAN YOU SEND
ME ALL THE NEWSLETTERS
THAT YOU HAVE WITH ALL
OF THE WORN UNDERWEAR
AND ALL OF THE VIDEOS
THAT YOU HAVE MADE
AND ALL OF THE LARGE
PHOTOGRAPHS AND ALL
OF THE PHOTOGRAPH
SETS THAT YOU HAVE
TO SELL FROM YOUR

PTO

3

FAN CLUB I HAVE
ENCLOSED A STAMPED
ADDRESSED
ENVELOPE WITH MY NAME
AND ADDRESS ON SO
YOU CAN SEND ME ALL
OF YOUR NEWSLETTERS
THAT YOU HAVE IT
WOULD MAKE ME SO VERY
HAPPY IT WOULD MAKE
MY DAY IF YOU WOULD
PLEASE SEND ME ALL
OF YOUR NEWSLETTERS
THAT YOU HAVE PLEASE
CAN YOU SEND ME YOUR
VALENTINE NEWSLETTER
FOR THIS YEAR AND PLEASE

PTO

4

CAN YOU SEND ME ALL OF
YOUR FULL LISTS AND ALL
OF YOUR NEWSLETTERS
THAT YOU HAVE AS FAST
AS YOU CAN PLEASE
WITH LOTS OF LOVE FROM
YOUR NUMBER ONE FAN

XXX

Felix

FELIX KNOWS THAT he is every young woman's dream, therefore he must be every young porn model's dream. Felix has it all – he is very wealthy. So wealthy in fact that he has his very own large country home, pool and jacuzzi (sorry 'jacousy'), yacht, riverside home and a permanent tan. He immediately made a bee-line for Shanine Linton, and proceeded to bombard her with erotic mail, suggestive mail and what I can only describe as 'art mail'. What Felix does is take the photos he has already bought from Shanine's Fan Club and mixes them with holiday photos of himself in a kind of accidental situationist/Jamie Reid style. He then takes photos of these new arty montages, and then sends these photos in to Shanine. These new images show the lovely Shanine in various states of sexual ecstasy with our brown Felix very much at the controls. Needless to say his constant home and hotel invites, and his frequent financial offers for sex (£400 for a night) result only in disappointment.

I STILL CAN READ IT... BUT STILL I DONT
KNOW ABOUT OUR "BUSINESS" DINER HA! HA!
I AM A BUSY MAN TOO... SO IT WOULD HELP
TO PLAN AHEAD... WHICH HOTEL (EXEPT. THE HILTON) DO
I GO THERE OFTEN
YOU LIKE BEST!

WOW I LIKE THE "OPEN CROUCH" ONE'S BEST AND
AS YOU CAN SEE IT MADE ME
SO HORNY I HAD "POSE" PUT INTO
ACTION AND PRESTO... FOUND
OUT HOW MUCH YOU LIKE
TO HAVE YOUR PUSSY EATEN
... MHH! THANK YOU LOVER!!
I LOVE YOUR VERY SENSITIVE
NIPPLES TOO... BUT ENOUGH FOR NOW!

SEND ME:
BRAND NEW SAUCY PHOTO SET } £ 15.00   SIGN... TO MY
    "   H/C BLUE   "   LOVER...
                                              S-
I WAS THINKING ABOUT THE DOLL, BUT
PREFFER THE REAL THING !!!!!!

                    TAKE CARE & THINK ABOUT OUR
DINER DATE!   (NORMALY I
              DONT ASK 2x)   LUV.

DEAR SHANINE,
I THINK YOU ARE
SUPER... JUST RIGHT
FOR THE SENSI-
TIVE CUDDLES!
I'M SINGLE
AND HAVE A
LOVELY COUNTRY
HOME WITH INDOOR SWIMMING POOL,
SAUNA & JACCOUZY AS WELL AS
A 260HP JACHT ON THE RIVER
COURE WHICH PETRUDS INTO
MY GARDEN!
I'M OF SWISS ORIGEN BUT LOVE
ENGLAND.
PERHAPS ONE DAY WE CAN MEET IN PERSON? WOULD
YOU LIKE TO JOIN ME AT THE HILTON FOR A NICE EVEN-
ING OUT, WHEN NEXT IN TOWN!
PLEASE FIND CHEQUE OF £35.00 FOR VIP MEMBERS
MY BIRTHDATE ████████

I'D A PERSONAL LETTER
PLEASE!

I KISS YOU GENTLY
ALL OVER.
LOVE,

I'll let you know
about dinner!
Shanine
x

Official Fan Club
Britain's sexiest Page 3 girl

SHANINE LINTON

c/o P O Box 56
Aldershot
Hants
GU11 3YX

Hi Lover,

A warm welcome to my fan club, sorry for the delay
with your bumper pack but I have been in Cyprus
with Page 3 photographer George Richardson shooting
a calendar for 1997.

I'm very busy at the moment as I am moving to
a new flat next week, it's taken me days to just
to get my frilly panties packed! I will be keeping
you posted of my antics, if you have any suggestions
regarding my fan club please drop me a line.

I look forward to hearing from you soon.

                    Love
                    Shanine
                    x

P.S. Sorry for the typed letter but my writing
is very messy!

HI SHANINE!
I PUT YOUR WORDS INTO ACTION...
AND ENJOYED IT VERY MUCH!!!
        YOU SEEM TO ENJOY
NUDITY & ARE PROUD OF YOUR BODY...
SO AM I (73KG)...NO BAD ISN'T!
(ALSO I AM IN A DIFF. FIELD THEN
YOURS.. ████████)
        HOW DO YOU LIKE
MY ARTWORK? (JUST FOR YOU!)
YOUR WRITING ISN'T MESSY..

67

I have never seen letters like this before. I find these letters fascinating, I don't know why exactly, I just do. So I start to collect them. I'm a natural-born collector, you see, on the fringes of autism I'd say, and I really can't help myself. My father collected. My mother collects. I collect. And these letters just have to be collected, by me. It could just be that I'm a colossal pervert, but for me the letters have a magic that I find difficult to describe. I read just as much as the next guy but I'm also very easily distracted when I am reading. But when I read these letters I am not distracted at all. They make me think about what the hell is going on in these people's lives and what the hell has gone on in their past. I wonder what they look like, I wonder what their homes are like, where they live and if the curtains are drawn as they write these steaming piles of filth. And so rather than see these letters disappear for ever into the bin, I start to collect them. I put them in my drawer at work. Every week, or when I remember, I empty the drawer, take the letters home and put them in a file.

8

THE REALLY ODD stuff can turn up at any time. I'm standing in the office as my sister opens a medium-sized, mysterious-looking parcel. It's off-square in shape, and wrapped up very well, with about half a roll of cheap imitation Sellotape, the type of tape that's just not very sticky and of a very thin gauge. All the stamps have plainly been nicked from an office somewhere because the £3 postal charges have been met with a whole sheet of 10p stamps. A pair of sharp scissors in my sister's experienced hand and this exciting gift is unwrapped for all to see. It's a squashed box of PG Tips. And inside the squashed box of PG Tips is a small and terribly ugly bear-cat-dog thing wearing a love heart. It is a most horrible-looking thing, but the thought, love and quite possibly passion that has gone into this gift is terribly sweet and touching. My sister and I spend a good half an hour giggling at the madness of it all, for these sorts of gifts are surprisingly regular. The girls also get sent a great number of old ladies' pants and stockings. Sometimes whole outfits appear: skirts, blouses, dresses and absolutely masses of perfume, mostly stolen testers. Lipsticks, jewellery – which are, as a rule, thin and goldy looking chains. Really horrid watches, as well as enormous and occasionally frightening-looking soft toys - the biggest so far being a three-foot Eeyore from *Winnie the Pooh*. Oh, and large amounts of strange chocolates, with brand names I have never seen before.

Not surprisingly, the girls don't want any of these things, so we start a monthly charity shop run where mother drives a large box of unwanted Fan Club gifts to the local Sue Ryder.

'And the latest Fan Club news darling is that another Fan Club is opening! How exciting is that!! Just think of all the sexy personal photos she has. Wow, you won't be able to control yourself!!' This is how I write to all the fans when we have big Fan Club news. It is about time my sister opened a new Fan Club, and so she does.

Vicky Lee (Fan Club No. 7)

COR BLIMEY! VICKY LEE. She looks like a mature, racy blonde vixen dolly thing, if you ask me. Trouble is that with the lovely Vicky Lee, we have lots of pictures of the new Pammy Anderson looky-likey Vicky Lee, but we also have lots of pictures of Vicky Lee way before the surgeon decided to get his knife out. As a result, if you buy the wrong Vicky Lee pictures, the ones depicting the younger, weirder-looking Vicky, you may think you have been sent photos of someone entirely different. There is the most enormous difference between the younger Vicky Lee, who looks much older, and the all-new older-but-much-younger-looking Vicky. And it's the all-new older-but-younger-looking Vicky Lee that the punters want – that's the all-new-older-Vicky with the classic Pammy Anderson looks, in case you are getting confused. And what a great plastic-like look Vicky bought for herself – perfect cheekbones, large pouty mouth, massive pointy knockers, shaved thighs, just like a giant sexy Sindy doll. So stunning is the all-new Vicky Lee, she manages to get herself the starring role in the famous Guinness 'Wedding' advert. Now I've said that, I'm not sure if it is that famous at all. Maybe that's my advertising past coming back to haunt me, but I know what commercial she's on about when she mentions it. Which she does a lot.

For Vicky and the other new girls, see pages 108-113.

9

WITH ALL THESE clubs – seven and counting – demand is high all the time. Demand for new photos. Demand for undies. And demand for sexy videos of all the girls. Photos and undies are easy. Videos are different. To start with, Eve sources new videos from elsewhere; some of the girls, Louise for example, have made videos in the past so my sister just buys them in and away they go to the fans. But we now have thousands of eager fans on the mailing lists, so my ever-resourceful sister decides to start her own video production company. She speaks to one of the better-known glamour photographers and together they put a couple of days aside and hold the first ever Eve Productions video shoot.

Eve organises everything because she seems more able and better suited to getting everything done than anyone else. Over a two-day period, she is the art director, set decorator, producer, financier, make-up artist – she does everything. She even stars in one of the videos herself.

Vicky Lee turns up on day one. The studio is in Camden, right in the middle of busy, urban London. Vicky Lee strolls up in thigh-length black rubber boots, skimpy blue rubber hotpants, a tiny skin-tight rubber squeezy booby top, enormous blonde hair, full porno make-up and not a lot else. She arrives at the studio in a state of shock, saying that she can't handle everyone on the high street staring at her. Poor girl.

On day two of the shoot I get a phone call asking about music. The films need music, but my sister has no budget available to spend on a composer or source music. She asks me if I can help because I tinker in music and she knows that for years I have collected vintage porn soundtrack recordings.

The truth of it is that I've been doing it since I was 15, I can't help it and it all started in a council house in Aldershot.

The gang of friends I hung out with at the time were all in this smelly house owned by someone's parents. It was a Saturday afternoon and Darren, the impressively tattooed 16-year-old gang leader, had dragged us all from the arcade to this tiny fleapit for a video-watching session. The curtains were drawn and the video was played. Lovely. Hardcore porn. Never seen it before in my life. All in German too. It was Darren's dad's naughty film. Or his stepdad's film. It may have even been his mother's film. I really can't recall. The gang sat there in the semi-darkness, giggling, watching, possibly learning and giggling some more. A couple of the gang were motionless and silent. But my memories of this first hardcore experience are not what you'd expect. I was turned on by the music, not the imagery. I'd never heard music like it before. All beats and throbs and grooviness. It pushed musical buttons in me that had never been pushed before. My quest had begun, a quest that would continue for years and take me to London and through vast international music mail order listings, and would, very slowly, set me on the road to my own collection of this rare and oh-so-prized music.

And now, pretty much for the first time since it all started, I feel like it's all coming together. Like a shot I go down to Camden, where the girls are shooting, and take a musical producer friend of mine along for the ride. His name is Pete and he makes psychedelic house music for a living. We get to the studio. Vida Garman is standing there, starkers. It's a shock for my musical friend Pete, but not for me as I've spent a long time now with naked-lady pictures and the best thing anyway in this situation is to just treat it as completely normal. Right, so we need some music. My sister plays us examples of what she wants; they'd been playing Bobby Brown while the girls had been stripping. They like Bobby's slow sexy funkiness. I look at Pete, the producer, he looks at me and we leave the little film studio in fits of laughter. We drive to Pete's music studio in Notting Hill, where we spent the next twelve hours putting together our interpretation of modern porn music. I've brought along several original dirty records like the *Deep Throat* soundtrack for inspiration, and we continue laughing solidly for a good ten of the twelve-hour session. It's a combination of the hilarious music and this ridiculous job that keeps us entertained so consistently.

As our session draws to a close, we find that we have produced several long, drifting tracks of what can only be described as porn-rocky house-funk. For added measure the tracks are punctuated with very camp synthesised strings and the odd kinky groan. A day later I pass the master CD to my sister, who is impressed enough with the music to send it immediately over to the editor and pay us a small fee for our trouble.

The editor. What a guy. We'll call him Harry. Harry is a man who has been editing porn in his front room for well over forty years. He's a pensioner. He's been editing all this time and his house is stacked with the very latest high-end editing gear, the latest transfer equipment, the newest in computer software and hardware and also, and best of all, one of the oldest vision mixers and video effects machines you've ever seen.

The result of his work, only a few days later, is magnificent. It appears to be a new kind of modern porn, a sex film mixed with the 'Bohemian Rhapsody' video, brilliant. The films all follow a basic premise. The girl introduces herself and says hello. For a few tense sexual seconds all is silent, before our groovy porn-rocky house-funk music breaks the silence. The camera is locked off in a bedroom scene, which my sister has decorated and dressed. The girl then appears stage left and over the next hour she strips twice. God is it dull. How long does it take you to take all your clothes off? Maybe one minute? And that includes hanging them all up too. Well, each single strip here takes half an hour. I feel sorry for the girls, having to wiggle about looking busy doing nothing for five minutes before the next item of clothing comes off. Hard work. And remember these are legal, soft videos. There is no naughty business here to fill up the time with. And every now and then there's a 'Bohemian Rhapsody' bit, where the image of the girl on screen will shrink down, then spin around and whizz off screen, leaving a trail of duplicated images behind it, which then fade to reveal another fresh picture of the girl in exactly the same scene as before. However, it's all good, solid commercial product for the Fan Clubs, the girls look great, the videos are well lit, nicely shot, and because they only show tits and bums they are easy to get certified.

As a bonus, if you decide to go for Louise's video you get some high jinks with a messy cream puff at the end.

The first series of Eve Productions videos are offered to the Fan Club members. Even if the content is pretty tame, the titles are all quite racy – *Red Hot Red Head* (Vida), *Virtual Sex* (Vicky Lee), *Sex Mag Model* (Louise Hodges), *Teenage Baby Doll* (Shanine) and *Porno Model* (Eve). The fans get excited and the videos fly off the shelves, and that means lots more work for everyone – me, my mother, Eve and Mr Patel.

73

10

Every three months we send out brand new newsletters to all the fans. These contain lots of new photos for the fans to buy. Three months later a whole new set of newsletters is written, with different new sets of photos and so on and so on. As soon as these new newsletters are sent out, we get lots of orders straight back in. Some of these new orders come back to us within a day or so, others within a week, others take a few weeks, and post dribbles in right up until it's time for the next brand-new mailing, which starts this cycle all over again.

Each club adheres to basic economic rulings. Diminishing returns, for starters. So what happens is that a Fan Club opens, and bam! There's this almighty explosion of interest. Hundreds of fans will join immediately. Then for every subsequent week fewer fans will join until after about two months just one or maybe two fans join a week. Then the first wave of newsletters and Fan Club packs will go out, and if we send out, say, 1,000 packs, something like 400 replies will be sent back to us within the first month. And then maybe another 100 will reply over the following month. So, in all, maybe half will eventually reply to each new mailing. Three months later, when the next new mailing goes out, there may only be a total of 300 replies to the newsletters. And so each Fan Club slowly diminishes over time.

Fans who join these clubs also settle nicely into one of three different groups:
1) you have the fan who joins and never buys anything that we offer;
2) you have the fan who joins and buys everything that we offer;
3) and lastly you have the fan who joins and may well buy something but it's anyone's guess when this might happen.

Because we know that a hefty whack of any Fan Club revenue is made at the beginning, when hundreds of new guys join, the future revenue is good but only over a long period of time. So it makes good business sense for my sister to open as many Fan Clubs as she can as often as she can.

And this is exactly what she keeps doing ...

Lana Cox (Fan Club No. 8)

FIRST UP IN the new batch is the lovely Lana Cox. A slightly exotic name for a slight, exotic woman from Russia. I don't know who she is and I don't know where exactly she's from, but Russia seems to be the word generally batted about. She is smaller than the average nudie, with a mouth full of teeth. It's her mouth, teeth and large gums that I always see first on a Lana picture, no matter what she is or is not wearing at the time. Lana works very hard. She does quite a lot of catalogue and undie work. She is a very pleasant young lady with a booming Eastern European voice and very little volume control. She is married to a man with a beard. He is English. Lana is good at looking very rude. Many of her photos are very rude. And because of her country of origin, she is often dressed up as a saucy spy from the KGB, in a military hat, kinky boots and not a lot else.

Belinda Charlton (Fan Club No. 9)

I REALLY DON'T know much about Belinda Charlton. She's a classic 90s Page 3 girlie with possibly a little late 80s thrown in. That's when she first started undressing, I believe. She is of medium build and she has average-size boobs which I would guess are enhanced but only a little. I also have no idea why my sister went for Belinda Charlton. I find all her photographs unbelievably plain and very dull. I suppose she is pretty and sweet-looking, perhaps a little wholesome, which might explain why she made so small a splash in the business. Very rarely does Belinda show anything but her boobs. And good for her for keeping it all for herself. The week we open her Fan Club, Belinda starts thinking about not being a glamour model any more, but we aren't too concerned because she has stopped being a glamour model before and then started again a few months later.

Teresa May (Fan Club No. 10)

NEXT UP IS Teresa May. It's a big Fan Club day when my sister makes a deal with the notorious Teresa May. Firstly she is very, very popular. Secondly her photos are amazing. Thirdly she's a right laugh and very up for all sorts of jobs and work. She's at it all the time. And as well as modelling full time she starts numerous businesses on the side, such as a model agency, then a printing company, that kind of thing. I admire Teresa's boundless energy. She has the perfect mind and body for the business of soft porn. She's had several boob operations. She is experienced in front of the lens and knows exactly what her fans want to see. When Teresa is naked and looking into the camera she knows what is going to happen when punters see the photos, and that's why she's so good. Teresa is the classic East London/Essex bird. She's very streetwise and is only in it for the money. Her biggest break to date, as well as being on numerous and pointless Kilroy-style shows and presenting on *Rude TV*, is her appearance as a naked wriggling girl in the notorious (and banned) 'Smack My Bitch Up' video by the Prodigy.

Teresa is surprisingly short for such a big UK porn star. Having met Teresa a few times I decide to get her in together with Pete, my music producer mate – the idea simply to make a bangin' house tune with Teresa singing either a suggestive or rude song. Good idea, I think. Sex always sells. However, we had no idea Teresa couldn't sing, and even with Pete's expensive, expansive modern studio equipment at our disposal we were unable to retune her voice or salvage anything usable from the vocals she spent three hours putting down. 'You can't polish a turd,' said Pete. So we got Teresa to talk dirty instead, which she is great at doing.

Samantha Jessop (Fan Club No. 11)

NOW I ALWAYS look at Sammy Jessop and think it's the frozen pea woman. That Patsy bird. Kensit. I think Sammy is a little taller, mind. Long legs, even longer in 4" stilettos. And Sammy has a great arse. And on the odd occasion when one doesn't find oneself looking at her arse, you notice that she has a very original porn star look – in the right situations Sammy Jessop visually smoulders with sex. The camera loves Sammy and she has made herself a success very quickly – the exotic shoots roll in for her. Like Lana, she does a fair bit of lucrative catalogue and underwear work. We have a good selection of sexy Sammy shots for the fans, but in amongst the extremely sexy ones are some slightly stranger Sammy ones, like Eighteenth Century-style sex shots with her wearing a massive powdered wig. I just don't get them at all.

Adele Stevens (Fan Club No. 12)

GOODNESS GRACIOUS. Adele Stevens. From Nottingham, I think ... And what a natural beauty she is. That's right, Adele is all natural – yes, boys and girls, those knockers are all real. Nothing is enhanced here. When I first met Adele I even asked her where she got her great body from. Apparently it comes from her mother. From our first delightful chat I discovered that Adele wants to work with animals, and her aim is to open an animal sanctuary. This is one of the sweetest things I've heard in the sex business to date. If you ask me, Adele looks like a movie star. She's simply stunning in photos. And just as beautiful in real life. She's one lovely girl, who I secretly think should not work in porn; she should be a veterinary nurse or something. But it would seem that there's more money to be made in getting your big boobs out. Of all the Fan Club girls to date Adele is the newest to the business and has become hugely successful and popular almost overnight. Which is exactly why our Eve signed her up.

I think it's a good idea now to quickly explain all these girls' photographs (*Meet the Girls, Part 2*: pages 108-113). These are great examples of what the Fan Clubs are selling to the fans. As you can see, they are simple but very well produced and professionally executed glamour shots. No rubbish for our Fan Clubs here.

I have to write descriptions of these very same shots for our newsletters as the girls have absolutely no intention of doing this job for themselves. All except for Eve, who describes her new shots to me in great detail.

And now that Sammy Jessop has opened a Fan Club with us I'd like to introduce another serial Fan. He starts writing to Sammy and my sister.

Mr. Mason

THERE'S NO-ONE QUITE like Mr. Mason. He'd been a quiet fan for quite some time, registered but dormant within my sister's club. But when Sammy arrives he really starts to communicate on a grand scale. It would also seem that Mr. Mason is a bit of a part-time calligrapher. He writes in a flashy script, but only on occasion. Sometimes he will write in his own form of hieroglyphics, or a horribly bastardised form of Sanskrit. Or in a witchy scrawl that he mixes with rune symbols. These peculiar scrawls appear on the back of envelopes, normally encircled by a large blotchy red line, probably drawn by placing a saucer on top of the envelope and drawing round it. There is something dark and vaguely ceremonial about it all, and my mother doesn't like these envelopes so she chucks them all away. Mr. Mason occasionally sends in very large parcels. Inside these large parcels are smaller parcels. Inside several progressively smaller parcels are sets of large white envelopes, all with these same red circles on.

Inside these envelopes are sets of smaller envelopes. All are opened (and this takes ages) to reveal nothing at all in any of them. Mr. Mason has also sent in dinner invitations to the Fan Club that we assume we have to then send on again on his behalf. I say send on because they are all sent to ladies who are nothing to do with the Fan Club at all, normally newsreaders, TV presenters, and pop stars from the 60s. I shall never forget his invite to dinner sent via us for Lena Zavaroni. Of course this tragic *Opportunity Knocks* mini diva died in 1999. Mr. Mason also writes in series, continuing themes over the course of his correspondence.

Mr. Mason has different ways of signing off. Here he uses something weird.

To : Belinda

Love
from
أَلْلُكِ رَجَل كِير

A typical Mr. Mason series. Expensive odd paper. All very carefully written in gold. And only he knows why.

Dear Lady Samantha,

Your

Password

is

" Professor. "

You are not to reveal your
Password to anyone.
No one knows your Password.
No one must ever know your
Password.
    I have given you this Password
for a reason and also this one.
    " Master King. "

with Deepest Love,

Dear Lady Samantha,

Your probably wondering what I meant so I'm going to tell you. This is what I mean. I. N. R. I. You will need to remember this. You are part of something very important. I will be most pleased when you get to use all of your talents. The reason why you are not able to do so, is already given above. It is safe to discuss this with Joanne Guest. I want you to remember this. No matter how much I explain you will not believe what is going to happen and you will never understand it. I believe, you already know something. I'll prepare you if you are not already prepared.

with Deepest Love,

Dear Samantha,

Thank you for your beautiful photographs. You work hard. I know you do.

You're a very talented young lady.

If there's anything worrying you, let me know. As long as I'm with you, you have nothing to worry about.

If I was alive you wouldn't need to be doing this.

In this time, you have to. Only in this time.

First place winner out of six. Thanks for telling me. I Love You

with Deepest Love,

82

Dear Eve,

You will get this after today. There are many things that I cannot tell you because of the nature of your work and there is a severe penalty for revealing what I know to those who don't. You have what you can handle. There are many things that I know that you cannot handle. However, enjoy your birthday and the less said the better. You will see why when the time comes.

with deepest love,

███████████████

11

AFTER THE SUCCESS of the first lot of sex videos, the time comes for the club to invest in a new series of productions for our ever-hungry patrons. My sister has realised we can shoot all these new videos at her home, so rather than hiring a professional and expensive cameraman and studio we hire two cameras, tripods, buy film, hire lights and a monitor and call in the girls for a day's shooting. Some of the girls are a little too busy on other assignments or just can't be arsed to make a video, so we are left with Louise, Teresa and Sammy as our willing and able-bodied models.

I've never shot a video before. Not a naked nudy one anyway. The cameras we hire are industry standard and, to my delight, dead easy to use. You turn them on, point at the naked lady and push 'Go'. My sister has conceived a shooting schedule and a way to get the maximum amount of videos for each girl out of a minimum amount of set-ups. Each girl will perform a solo shoot in the office, in the kitchen, in the bedroom and in the bathroom. This gives us more than enough footage for the standard solo girl videos. Then we can also compile the best bits from the various shoots together to give us themed multi-girl videos. Simple. However, nothing ever goes as planned. Some of the girls turn up late. No problem, we'll cope. Teresa turns up driving like Penelope Pitstop with the roof down on her convertible Beemer, and it's only when she screeches to a halt that I see she is still wearing curlers in her hair. They are big and blue. She looks mad. The girls all in, we sit and chat with tea and biccies in the kitchen, discuss briefly what needs to be shot in the time we have, then it's down to business.

We begin in the office, and the girls take it in turns to look like bored yet horny secretaries who then strip very slowly in front of their desk. One of our cameras is locked off with a wide shot, and I'm using the other camera to get some of the more intimate shots that the punters seem to like. Intimate is, I think, the wrong word to use here. I take close-ups of the girls' mouths. And their ears. Their fingers. Their legs. As the strip plods on – it takes half an hour, remember – the girls have to get extremely inventive. We have a ruler in the desk drawer which adds a little entertainment and distraction for about three minutes. We have a phone on the desk. This distracts for a further five minutes because when each girl picks up the receiver she can and always will pretend it's a dirty phone call. There is no talking in the finished films so these dirty phone calls are totally silent. Quite weird to see live, a girl on the phone half naked and miming rude words. But on video it all looks suitably exciting and rude. We have a big filing cabinet too, and the girls can waste a good four, or maybe even five minutes opening and closing drawers and pretending to file things away. Oh, and one other thing, because the girls are playing at horny secretaries, they all have to wear glasses. Glasses are very good props. Firstly they confirm immediately that the girl is definitely a secretary, and just the process of taking them off, sliding them back on and then taking them back off again, effortlessly gets rid of another few video minutes. As we reach the twenty-five-minute mark, each girl is normally down to her knickers. These then take a further four minutes to slide off, so you can imagine the weird jiggling, bending and wiggling that has to go on. Once they're off, it's all over, girl trots off naked, we stop filming and prepare ourselves for the next secretary to arrive. It's all good clean fun. That is until Louise arrives, ready and willing for her naughty office strip. Now, Louise is a naturally rude young lady, so we constantly have to stop her being too explicit with the ruler and dirty with the phone receiver, but at least her shoot adds a little variation.

Next location is my sister's kitchen, for some very horny housework. And we're rapidly running out of time. Same slow strips as before, different room, and this time with brooms, dusters, cloths and mops all adding to the narrative. Louise improvises by adding lots of tap rubbing and bending over for dropped J-cloths.

Finally, we just have enough time to head upstairs and into the bathroom. The bathroom shoots are harder to film because there is hardly any space at all for two cameras, me and a stripping girl. But they are far easier for the porn stars. We all know girls are quite used to splashing about in the bath for well over half an hour, so these videos are a breeze. The girls can strip fairly fast, say about five minutes, and then spend the next twenty-five minutes soaping, rubbing, shaving (armpits and legs only please, Louise), shampooing, before climaxing with lots of over-excited rinsing and a final vigorous towelling off. These are the only scenes that I find particularly difficult. Look, I'm a man and I like sex. I also really like boobs. And as I'm filming in intense close-up of these wet and soapy bathroom boobs, my mind begins to wander in the wrong direction. I get very hot. The bathroom gets very hot. I defy anyone not to get a little confused and altered while filming a top glamour model slowly soaping and rubbing her big knockers inches from your face. For a full ten minutes. It's not easy. And Sammy Jessop has brought this strange white spongy thing with her that creates even more lather than before and she rubs her pert tanned boobs very slowly indeed for ages and ages and all the expensive soapy lather dribbles everywhere slowly and it all gets really hard for me. Difficult to film, I mean.

When we're all wrapped up and dry again and the girls have left for home, Eve and myself discuss the day's filming. Maybe we could have done with another cameraman so we have even more footage to play with. Maybe next time. But a few days later when the films have been sent to our faithful editing OAP, he calls to say the footage is most excellent and some good videos will be forthcoming. So my sister is happy, her home-made video gamble has paid off so far, now she just has to get the videos finished, named, certified and then she can sell them everywhere. And because these are soft videos, not only can the Fan Club sell them but so can all the UK sex shops and even stores like HMV in their very tame adult video section.

The resulting videos – *Sex Mad Secretaries*, *Horny Housewives on the Job* and *Hot Wet Shavers* prove to be an instant success. It's the titles that do it every time, you see. And Eve is good at titles. You may have the most spectacular sex video to sell but if the title is poor and doesn't conjure up filthy sex images in the mind of the prospective buyers then it won't sell.

With these early successes under her belt, it's not long before Eve has organised some more simple strip films for me to shoot. First up is the lovely Adele. Phwoor! Exciting. This will be her first ever video. Her naked debut. My sister gets in some champagne, which kind of suits Adele's movie-star looks, and also gives her a bucket of ice. The ice and the phallic bottle make the thirty-minute strip in my sister's front room a little easier to deal with. I mean, it whizzes by. You can play with ice for ages. And sure enough Adele rubs the top of a champagne bottle for quite a while too. She's a bit keen with this stripping lark, and actually begins the whole strip with hardly anything on at all. So, within twenty minutes she's naked, she's already played with the champagne bottle and we still have ten minutes left to run. We improvise as best we can, and Adele spends this time drinking more champagne naked, gazing out of the window naked and then rolling around on the floor naked. It's ridiculous but no one cares at all. She looks lovely all the time and that overrides the stupidity of her rolling around nude on the carpet for no real reason at all.

After this first strip and following a quick check for carpet burns, we get Adele on the horny housewife tip and I film her hoovering naked, which is something I never thought I'd see in a million years. We call Adele's very tame debut video *Swedish Sex*. This is a good, if not great, title from my sister. However, Adele is not Swedish, my sister's house is in Bucks, and there is no sex anywhere in the film. But it's still a great suggestive title, which is all important.

Next up on Eve's new, inventive video list is a bit of lesbianism. The fans like a bit of this, and it also means you can get members from two girls' clubs potentially buying the same video – clever, eh? So we get back Teresa May to the house and she is joined this time by Louise Hodges. They have worked as lesbians before on numerous other shoots. They're not real lesbians, just very convincing professional porn actresses who get along well. For this fabulous new big-budget production they are going to be nurses. So it's a lesbian nurse thing, which is great because it's different. As far as props are concerned we have a set of toy Doctor and Nurse things, specifically a large yellow plastic toy syringe which will not be used for anything on this video and a red and blue plastic stethoscope which will be used a lot. Plus a large paper and plastic thermometer. The girls are both wearing those trashy nurse outfits from Ann Summers and massive black patent leather stilettos which I'm sure would be banned on a real hospital ward. As usual I am filming with a locked-off camera and a hand-held intimate one and together these girls make fabulous fake lesbians. There's a lot of licking and rubbing and sucking, all with pants on. The resulting video, *Lesbian Student Nurses*, is yet another good seller. Things are looking mighty fine for the Fan Clubs, and the new video business my sister has developed is proving profitable quickly – and is all terribly good fun for me. The fact that I have no formal film training or video experience does not matter here. As I believe a young Roman Polanski once said, film technique is not important when you are shooting pornography. Or something along those lines anyway.

12

IT'S ABOUT THIS time that the phenomenon known as 'table dancing' starts invading our shores. We all are aware of the old-fashioned seedy strip clubs, but this table dancing lark is a new and very American invasion. It is destined to revolutionise dead boozers and dying nightclubs up and down the country. The deal is simple: men come in and sit down, girls dance erotically on tables right in front of them, and the more the men pay at the table, the more is revealed by the girl. It's a bit like going out to a restaurant, paying for an expensive meal and very nearly getting something to eat. Because of the close proximity of the girls the thrills are instant and very real, and cash changes hands quickly. There is also the opportunity, depending on the venue, to have solo dances with a dancing girl. This looks ridiculous and a bit like a strange form of torture, which it is I suppose. The paying victim sits on a chair, hands by his side or crossed, the naked girl then wiggles and wobbles all around him for about five minutes, and that's about it. And it's expensive. This new phenomenon is a cash cow for all the glamour and porn girls willing to dance erotically in public, and most begin to capitalise on it right away. New table dancing venues start springing up every week. One such venue is the Circus Tavern. And where is the Circus Tavern? In the middle of nowhere. In a place called Purfleet, a lovely town in Essex. The actual building is a mad 60s block of concrete on the dead side of Dagenham. It's massive. They've packed out darts championships there. It's a watering and entertainment hole that holds 2,000 or more. This delightful nightspot quickly becomes the largest table dancing venue in 'London'. The owner, a slick, perma-tanned ex-wrestler by the name of Paul Stone, blessed with the looks of a young Peter Stringfellow, is a well-connected businessman. With the help of the *Sport* newspaper he organises the biggest, bounciest table nights in the land. That's 2,000 men and about 75 wild ladies all thrown together right in the middle of nowhere. The Fan Club somehow gets involved in this big whoop-up, and when the nights are established and running well my sister believes that it's the perfect place to promote the clubs and to make a bit of money with all the girls.

Her idea is simple. Both Eve and Donna do not dance. Well, they do, but not naked on tables in front of men. They are top porn stars, so maybe they're above it all. They decide to make special guest appearances at this exciting night out. Appearances with a lucrative twist. They will roam around this massive venue, promote the clubs, give out membership leaflets and have Polaroid pictures taken with their adoring fans, a tenner a go. For this night's work Eve and Donna will need help, so yet again I am enlisted, but we do still need another pair of hands. I call my good friend Delby. He's perfect for the job. Delby is an interesting man. He's a talented graphic designer. However, I'm convinced he spends most of his working day thinking about sex and making large donations into his wank bank. He's also well known amongst my small circle of friends for getting into all sorts of unusual sexual situations. A good example is when he has sex with someone's wife while the husband sits back, looks on and films. That kind of thing. He's also well known for the content of sexual post he gets sent on a regular basis from his small bevvy of regular shags – 'My cunt, your cock, tonight' being one of the more memorable letters received. It's all a little strange because Delby looks like John Denver, not the looks you'd necessarily associate with a lively sexual adventurer. Anyway, I call him and naturally Delby is well up for the job in hand.

Together we drive to the Circus Tavern. It's a very wet Friday. There are many commuter-based jams. We talk about graphic design and sex on the long, slow car journey. We still manage to arrive early at the Tavern and are shown backstage, straight into the ladies' changing room. This is all a little shocking for Delby; he may be entirely used to a variety of strange sexual experiences and brief encounters, but to stand in a room full of well over fifty porn stars, almost all of whom are naked, is a little too much.

I know some of the girls quite well and this is work for me so their nakedness is not a problem or distraction. The girls all relax and get on with their shaving, pouting, tweaking and chatting. I notice there are a lot of high boots being worn tonight. That's the thing with porn stars, they all wear the same thing – one girl starts wearing high glittery kinky boots with a glittery bikini one week, I guarantee you that they'll all be wearing it the next week. It's exactly the same with tattoos and body jewellery. One gets her belly button pierced, and bang! They're all at it. Anyway, we get our instructions for the night from my big sister. The plan is that while the dancing is going on Eve will take one side of the venue, Donna the other, we will tour the tables where there are no dancers and ask if anyone wants a personal photo with either of the girls. We have boxes of Polaroid film, cameras, pens (for signing) and leaflets. I'm to go out with Donna, and Delby will escort Eve. There's a slight problem with Donna, though. She wants to make some money tonight, realises she has to go topless to really cash in, and then decides she doesn't want to do it at all. Maybe it's all an attention-seeking thing, but with a little head to head all is sorted and the idea of making double or treble what she might make fully clothed pushes all the right buttons. Delby and I leave the hot and highly perfumed changing room and go to survey the Tavern bars. This place is huge. I mean massive. And all the bouncers are just as large. I then notice on a wall by a bar a sizeable framed shot of Bernard Manning giving us all the bird. I look around. There seem to be hundreds of large tables, full of men drinking. No women anywhere. The bars – and there are at least four of these – are crowded with men drinking quickly. Everywhere I look there are men with trays full of wobbling pints trying to find their mates and table. There is a buzz of sexual anticipation in the room. It's like a bustling meat market before the meat has arrived.

Still an hour to go. The drink is really flowing, and the atmosphere grows in intensity. The hours pass, the drink is still flowing freely and the anticipation reaches a raucous boiling point. Throughout the venue, men are craning their necks looking for naked girls. But the girls keep them all waiting for as long as possible. It's now past eleven and the lights in the venue are dimmed. Cheap pop house starts pumping from the huge sound system. It's very loud. A compere comes to the stage, shouting through an over-amplified mike. He explains the house rules: no touching allowed. You will be removed if you start touching. Hands below the table at all times. He then introduces all the girls one by one. They all come out looking like a depraved, failed bunch of old American cheerleaders. And out they run into the maze of tables and men. The house music pumps louder, the girls make deals at the tables, cash changes hands and the dancing begins everywhere. Each dance is about three or four minutes, the length of each track, then all the girls change tables. I start with Donna, walking around the venue. Delby starts with Eve in the opposite direction. 'Topless picture with Donna, sir? Only a tenner.' There are no takers to begin with. Then someone bites. He hands over his tenner and stands smiling next to a tall topless Donna; I take the instant photo and Donna signs it for him. Like the old street trader tactic, this first punter makes all the others a little braver, and immediately we are surrounded by guys all wanting their own personal picture and, occasionally, a lucky peck on the cheek. We carry on wandering around the venue, servicing these keen young men. I look around and all I see are bums, tits and other parts of naked sweaty, preened female wobbling and gyrating in every direction. I have never seen anything like it in my life, and with the loud incessant banging of house music the venue is transformed into some modern bacchanalian scene. Everyone sweats: the girls, the punters, and me with my camera. The massive bouncers keep a beady eye on everything – this venue even has bouncers in cages above the crowds. No one gets away with anything in here.

A quiet-looking man approaches. He asks me for help. Where is Shanine Linton? he asks. I look at him and notice he is clutching a handful of Shanine newsletters. I'm afraid she's not here tonight, I reply. It seems this dedicated fan has come all the way from the north of England hoping she'd appear. He looks very out of place, in a smartish jacket and trousers; he looks nervous. I suggest he writes to her at the club to find out where she may be dancing or appearing. He lets me get on with my Donna job. He asks me all the same questions half an hour later round the corner. He also puts an 'r' in her name (Sharnine) every time he says it.

As the night bangs on it becomes obvious that there are a large number of punters who have failed to get any girls dancing in their area. They are on a slightly raised platform to the side of the main floor and bars. They keep coming over to me, telling me to get girls for them, and I explain that it's not my job. I try and explain this to one guy but he's sozzled beyond belief and has psychotic eyes that aren't looking in my direction as we converse. Donna and I move on, taking more expensive Polaroids. I have two cameras on the go at the same time so no one gets missed or has to wait. And I'm already running out of film. All of a sudden there's a disturbance in the room, and a rushing of large bouncers in the general direction of the raised platform. The next few minutes are like something from the OK Corral, with chairs, tables and men flying all over the place. Everything is getting smashed up. I rapidly escort Donna backstage, where we meet Delby, my sister and a large number of the sweaty table dancers. We watch the brawl from a safe distance, and it's only a matter of maybe two minutes until the offending men have been beaten out of the venue. The house music continues, the girls continue as if nothing has gone on, the drinking carries on and we finally stop taking pictures when we're all out of film. Back to the dressing room and we work out the money made over the last few hours. The girls get the lion's share. We get good money for having helped out, and some stories to tell. Delby's wank bank account has received handsome new deposits.

We take a last look at the obscene scene, the living carnage that's still going on, say goodbye and quickly exit the Tavern. The gravel car park is strewn with table-dance casualties, men with their heads down and their pockets empty. There are guys throwing up all over the place. Sexual tension is everywhere tonight; I'm sure it won't be long before another brawl begins. We find the car and leave Purfleet quickly. We get a speeding ticket on the way home.

The very next week, thanks to my collection of porn-related recordings, I get asked to DJ at a sex party. Ever the adventurer, I say yes. I call up Delby again, and he's more than happy to tag along, help carry my records and maybe 'get involved'. We drive towards the party. We follow the *A–Z* and find ourselves outside an enormous but seemingly abandoned house in Hampstead Garden Suburb. We park, grab the records, and stroll inside. We look incredibly normal. The place is full of men and women very much in touch with their sexual preferences, and proud to display it. There are people tied up everywhere and apparently loving it. Others are either masked or topless, but the atmosphere remains exciting and groovy, not dark at all.

We are shown upstairs, past a giant, eight-foot-tall washing machine. On the front is a slot. Put a pound in the slot, the pony-printed curtain on the front of the washing machine parts, and in front of you is revealed a large round magnifying glass. Behind this glass is a naked lady. She is contorting her privates for all to see. It's a very 'funny' party. I go upstairs and play sex records in the groovy relaxing area. People in leather jockstraps are coming and going. In between my records, the sound of spanking emanates through the walls. Delby is busy being voyeuristic. I play for a couple of hours, get groped from behind a few times, then meet the next DJ who will take my place. She's a typical, and quite beautiful, Jewish Princess. She arrives looking smart in a white shirt and black skirt, carrying her record box but no headphones, which is a sin in DJ circles. A few minutes later I turn around and she is starkers; she has very large breasts and even larger bolts piecing each nipple. Nothing is normal tonight. Delby and I wander the party for a little longer, we realise we are overdressed and a little out of place. Delby watches the washing machine for a bit. I watch my records. We leave when we realise the lavatories are broken.

This is Elvis, the unluckiest guy in the world. He tried to go to a table dancing night.
A brilliant and touching piece.

92

MEM NO VOO971

26.).

To my Darling teddy bear,

hi sexy vider. I hope
you're fine and in goal health.
I'm Sorry I haven't wrote to you for a long
time but I haven't been very well Since i got
beat-up in October last year on my way to a
table top dancin' at Boyds nightclub in Hockley
BIRMINGHAM. You See I was waiting for a train
at the time when 5 yobs attacked me Just for
minding my own buisness if that's Justice then it
stinks honey. One of them Said that's what you
get for tryin to look like that fat git Presley.
The Cops Caught them and locked them up and all
they got was a fine and a Slap on the wrist.

If anything it's made me more determined to keep my hair black and grow my sideburns after they cut them off. I just feel so mad and angry that if a person can't wear their hair they want to then it's a sad world darlin' you know what i mean.

I'm sorry if i seem so bitchy but that's the way i feel anyway on to some good news i'm on the road to recovery now.

And i swear to God that i'm determined to come and see you at Birmingham when are you there next?

You are so sexy you turn me on just lookin' at your pictures and photo's you're so beautiful you shine. You're eyes are like the ocean, you're so God damn horny, your lips are beautiful to kiss over and over again and your body God what a body i could and would die for you you're a sex coless honey oh yeah! before i forget are you going to sell your love dolls or your Pussy again as my last doll was Knicked yes I had my flat broke into again i must be the most unluckiest guy in the world.

I still think you're the loveliest woman on this Planet infact even more than the whole wide world.

It will be valentines day Soon and i'm gonna do you a love Song tape of me Singing because my love for you is so Strong that it hurts because i Can't have you never mind i'll Just Pretend that you're by my Side every mornin' and every night.

By the way how is Christopher give him a big hug and a Kiss and Say Elvis Say's hello for me.

And if you thought i forgot about you think again no Chance my love for you will go with me till the day i die because you're so special to me

Ever Since i first Saw your Picture in the
Paper I Said to my self i could quite easily
go to bed with that lovely girl You've got
Sex appeal darlin with a Capital S i could
Kiss you from head to toe and back up again
the front and the back.
Anyway Sweetheart tell Sharline and Eve
that i'll write to them Soon and tell that
lovely Liz williams to run a fan club She's
another horny girl You two would make a
great Picture together.
Anyway my darlin teddybear time to dream
about you and your lovely body and hope to
hear from you Soon

for ever yours

Your Number 1 fan

Elvis.

X X X X X X X X X X X X X X X X X X X X X X X X
X X X X X X X X X X X X X X X X X X X X X X
X X X X X X X X X X X X X X X X X X X X X X X
X X X X X X X X X X X X X X X X X X X X X X X

13

DELBY IS A trusted friend of mine. He's exactly the kind of mate I need to talk to now about collecting all these letters. I try and explain why I'm hoarding them. I try and work out why I'm doing it and exactly what to do with them all. It concerns me. I worry about it all. By now my collection of fan mail has grown considerably, and just about every week I add more. I keep most of the serial mail and also anything that comes in that catches my eye. My mother regularly lets out shrieks of horror from her desk as either a new racy letter or obscene photo pops out of its envelope. These little shrieks are like a calling for me, and I immediately investigate the cause.

So the collection grows, and at the end of a week I'll empty my drawer of new letters and take them home. Either that, or they'll sit in my bag in a file on the off chance I might bump into a mate. If I do and the vibe is right, and we're in the right, quiet environment I'll get the new letters out, try and explain what I'm doing, hand the letters around one at a time and wait for some kind of feedback. This is when it starts getting interesting. The reaction to the letters is quite incredible. Everyone I show them to wants to see more and read more. Sometimes people are shocked. Sometimes they laugh. Sometimes they're just bewildered. More often than not the letters will start a whole evening's conversation on the business of pornography, the whys and the why nots of it all. But every time I show letters to someone, they always want to see more. I start using these little revealing sessions to try and work out what on earth I'm doing with the letters in the first place, and what on earth I might do with them in the future. My collecting continues, as does my sister's. She now collects Fan Clubs and it's only a matter of time before two more clubs are founded, making a grand total of fourteen in all. Things are starting to get confusing and on top of it all, it looks like my sister is going to up sticks and move again.

Linsey Dawn McKenzie (Fan Club No. 13)

IT'S NOT DIFFICULT to see why Linsey Dawn McKenzie has become such a successful porn model so fast. She has all the right qualifications. She is a very rude young lady. She is very good looking if you like that kind of thing. She has the biggest, pertest natural boobs I have ever seen. And she's young, so they still defy gravity. The first time you see a Linsey Dawn shot, you can't help but gawp. Like many of the other girls, Linsey is streetwise and intends to make as much from porn as she can. She goes out with footballers and TV soap stars. She'd love to be as successful as Jordan, but isn't. Linsey is a short woman, and the first time I saw her my immediate thought was that the circus must be in town. She was wearing very high stilettos and was still short and looked even more mad because of the overall massiveness of her top half. I just couldn't believe she could walk upright. Linsey has sweet, sexy pictures taken, but occasionally she goes for it and has really rude pictures taken. By the time she joined my sister's organisation she had already forged quite a career for herself and had managed to make a fine series of Big Boob videos for people like 'Double D Productions' who specialise in freakish mammary porn. She'd also made a lesbian feature with her 'cousin', one with her less blessed sister, a couple of schoolgirlie ones on her own and even one with her old boyfriend, which is hilarious. When it arrives in stock I watch it to see how they can get away with 'genuine' hardcore boy/girl sex and still produce a softcore video. A quick viewing on FFWD reveals that the trick is simple: Linsey does loads of close-up snogging with her boyfriend around the house and in the garden. But when it comes to anything explicit the two of them would either be round the corner going 'ooh, aaah' a lot, or up the stairs and out of sight, or at the other end of the garden so far away that you can sort of maybe see they're at it but just can't be too sure. Quite simply a terrible video. Linsey also has a tattoo that says 'Mum' on her arm.

Alison Amberley (Fan Club No. 14)

THIS IS ANOTHER young porn lady I'm unfamiliar with. Never heard of her. But all of a sudden, and probably thanks to her 'sex tour of Britain', Alison Amberley has become very popular. Looking closely at the endless *Sport* articles about this 'country-wide sex tour', it's plain to see (if you look hard enough) that in most of the photos Alison isn't in Barnsley or Cardiff or wherever she's supposed to be, she was just pasted onto the relevant location picture, and normally out of scale. Maybe she did really do the tour, but either way she's now hot. Another model who's been surgically enhanced, Alison had done quite a lot of soft but quite explicit photo work a few years ago, none of which is available now. We've had some new photos done but there aren't that many of them, and they're all pretty much the same: a picture of Alison, front-on and topless in a miniskirt. This for me is a nightmare, as to describe Alison topless again and again in yet another miniskirt gets really difficult, especially if you want to make it exciting enough for fans to purchase. So I'll have Picture One: Alison in a sexy and really tight green miniskirt! 'And green is my fave colour!!' Sexy!! Picture Two: Alison looking incredibly horny and dying for sex, totally topless and in an amazing dusty pink miniskirt!! Wow!!! Picture Three: This is just the best shot ever! It's a BRAND NEW SHOT of Alison TOTALLY NAKED except for a really lovely new miniskirt!!! 'I bought it the other week and I know you'll love how I look in it!!!' See what I mean? It's not easy. And just as she joined up she finished her so-called sex tour of Britain, and then buggered off to France.

The two new clubs open with the usual bang so it's all go again, with Christmas approaching, swiftly followed by Valentine's …

It's during this Christmas that we have an unusually big family get-together. Mother, Big and Little Sister, and me. We don't get together that often, and there aren't many in the family. David, my sister's man, takes us all out for a Christmas feast at the Ritz. It's all very flash. I get to wear my charity-shop tuxedo at last. One of the few special guests my sister brings along is an old and very good friend of David Sullivan, John East. He's an entertaining and charismatic gentleman with a well-established naughty streak. I sit with him throughout dinner. He's spent much of his life involved with London nightlife. He's got keys to all the strange London clubs that don't exist any more. Back in the 60s he'd been the London chaperone to visiting Hollywood stars, he'd be in charge of their evening's entertainment, and my night was spent listening to his choicest stories about very famous people, most of whom are female. John East also had a more curious upbringing than most, as the adopted son of Max Miller, the most famous of all cheeky chappies. John had spent his entire youth as a stooge in the music halls and his conversation is pitted with old-fashioned rude jokes and is hugely entertaining. I think he misses the good old days of dashing between London theatres. John East also knew Mary Millington. They were good friends right up until she died.

We talk about my work, antiques and my enthusasm for old pornographic recordings. 'I've got one,' he tells me. A few weeks later I take delivery of a Mary

Millington tape, a recording she used to sell at her own sex shop in Tooting in the 70s. Apparently, Mary used to run her shop wearing only a bikini. She'd obviously made the recording at home, talking about her numerous sexual exploits on Side One and then urinating in the bathroom for all to hear on Side Two, before playing with her favourite vibrator for a memorable finale. It seems like the recording was made in a couple of days and nights; the quality is beyond dreadful and I'm convinced Mary was battered on cocaine throughout most of it because of the way her jowls seem to stick as she talks in her hokey-cokey way. But there's something strikingly humble, sweet and endearing about the whole tape and the way she talks about herself and sex. John East gives me permission to issue this recording on vinyl, and a couple of months later I release 'Come Play Me ... Mary Millington Talks Dirty' as a record for the first time. I only press 1,000 copies and they all sell in a week. Obviously I am not the only one in the world who looks out for porn-based recordings. I would have made a few quid on the sales but a graphic artist ran away with the profits. Don't ask me why.

Christmas passes in its usual frantically busy fashion, and the new orders still keep coming in well into January. Time to write the special loved-up Valentine newsletters for all the girls. And since the girls are a nightmare to communicate with, there is less news to write about and more photos for sale. Now Valentine's is probably more important than Christmas at the Fan Clubs, so we have to do something a little special for the fans. Offer them something a little out of the ordinary. This is never easy. I normally have to go out and find some special knickers or something like that for the girls.

I'm having my hair cut at the barber's again, and while we're talking about sexual mail order (a subject my hairdresser, Craig, is fascinated by), he mentions a gay friend of his in Germany who's been selling panties and pubic hair via magazines and mail order. Apparently this guy didn't know any girls, but that hadn't stopped him selling worn panties and pubic hair. Craig finds it all terribly funny because the guy was using his own hair and beard for the job. And when he'd run out of that he'd used the stuffing from an old horsehair mattress. He'd even used beard cuttings that Craig had sent over from London. This continental geezer was charging a fortune to randy Europeans and getting away with it, and it gave me an idea. Back at the office I discussed the pubic hair issue with my sister. She'd already had several requests (as had most of the girls) for pubic hair, and had occasionally cut and supplied a bit for the right price. I suggested she took a risk and allowed me to place this precious treat on her special Valentine mailing. She was quite happy to snip and sell it until she ran out. As a result I place this item for sale in her new mailing as a strictly limited edition – first come, first served.

The letters went out. Fewer men went for it than I first imagined. Maybe hair is just a German thing? They don't do under their arms over there, do they?

Right in the middle of this whole Valentine's madness, my sister moves. Again. This time she uproots to Essex as her relationship is blossoming and child number two is on the way. What with my pregnant sister's mood swings and mountains of work from the new Fan Clubs, more than ever I start to wonder where exactly my life is – or rather, isn't – going. And in this situation the last thing you need to be doing is replying to complaints, dealing with ridiculous queries, answering yet another Trevor begging letter and so on. So, me and my sister have our first ever argument. It's been brewing and is all about very little. I want some kind of commission for coming up with the idea of selling my sister's pubic hair. What a revolting thought. It didn't even work as an idea but I have a big buzzing bee in my bonnet about it all, I reckon I deserve about £30 extra for the week, but my sister is having none of it, and so a brief and explosive slagging match begins and ends with my sister slamming lots of doors, and a short period of refection for me. Once I've calmed down, I realise that I'm lucky to have such a simple, free and easy job almost whenever I want it; it pays me money and also allows me to explore other avenues at the same time. I even film naked ladies as part of the deal. Having my cake and eating it alone is something I rarely try these days.

Once this brief Valentine shenanigans has died down and my sister has uprooted herself and the office to Essex, we switch to video mode again. Eve's new home needs restoration, so we have no studio. Instead, my sister employs a guy she knows (who has been filming 'birds' for a few years now) to go and film one of the notorious Circus Tavern table-dancing monster nights. Most of the Fan Club girls are there shaking their bits all over the shop, and *Naked Table Dancing Extravaganza* is the resulting video. Badly lit, terribly shot, the one redeeming feature for most of the fans seems to be the 'up the skirt' action that appears midway through this audio-visual mess. This is now fashionable. Yes, let's film up porn stars' skirts and see if they are wearing knickers or not. I think it's all about being a naughty boy, if you know what I mean; a bit of nostalgia. Maybe I'm wrong. Yes, I am wrong.

While we wait to set up the new Essex office, I move all the equipment, desks, files, the huge plans chest, all the leaflets, newsletters, knicker boxes, videos and shelving into a large and very cold storage barn. Even in the summer it's cold, but radio reception is good and there is lots of space, which makes it easier to send out the masses of videos being ordered. I can also watch the birds (mainly greenfinches) being all territorial outside on the rosehip hedges that surround the barn. Mother is still working away a couple of times a week, mainly opening and sorting a large portion of the mail that pours in relentlessly. She is getting fairly efficient at it all, and is even occasionally taking it upon herself to make decisions as to what is and what is not acceptable for the girls and the Fan Clubs. As you might imagine, the girls get special requests from fans. Many of these are fairly normal, like 'Could you please sign this picture I found of you that was in last week's Sport newspaper?' However, some of the requests are a little more bizarre, and occasionally obscene. In these cases, my mother takes action. She reaches into her drawer and pulls out the pad of mini post-it notes. On these she writes what she thinks. The letters are then passed on to me for further action. Normally I write back a letter explaining that the request is a little too much for the girls to deal with, or I don't reply at all if the fan in question has already been told this once and is trying it on again.

As well as the occasional obscene request, any number of filthy photos can arrive at any time. These are very unpredictable. They are not normally like Geoffrey's Big Rising Willie portrait. They are far stranger, and most of these obscene or disastrous photos are immediately destroyed (unless, of course, there's a special request by the fan to return all photos). They tend to be self-portraits of fans, normally with very proud erections, normally very out of focus and for some reason, as Eve always points out, shot next to the cooker. As well as these grotesque, graphic self-portraits, there are others taken in front of mirrors, usually from a distance. Here the offending fan will be sat on the floor of his bedroom, naked, holding a camera and with his legs wide apart. The resulting photos are not too impressive, as you might imagine: you get naked legs, maybe a head if you are lucky and then just a giant flash over the area the fan really wants us to see, as the light just reflects back from the mirror when the photo is taken. We see these over-exposed flash photos regularly. It seems to be a common problem that the fans can't seem to solve. Then there are the really naughty shots sent in, of wives and/or girlfriends naked and playing with themselves in one way or another. Not nice. I shall never forget an anonymous set sent in of an old lady up to no good in a caravan.

We settle down to business in the barn with no heating and I realise that I enjoy spending the day working on my feet, as opposed to being sat at a desk. I seem to be more efficient this way. Work goes well and as winter approaches and the greenfinches raid the last of the rosehips my sister gives birth to Son Number Two. Eve seems to work throughout the arrival of the new baby, constantly on the phone sorting out business, when really she should be taking it easy. But oh no, not Eve. She's not like that at all, not if there's work to be done.

The old house she has just bought slowly comes to life, and as soon as it's ready for her to move into we get straight back to making videos, which are still the most lucrative line in the Fan Club business. For some time now Eve has been negotiating a deal to get Donna 'The Body' Ewin to expose her divine curves on video for her fans one final time. It's looking like Donna's retirement from the business is approaching very fast, and as soon as she passes The Knowledge she's going to be off, fully clothed for ever in her shiny black cab. So a deal is done, a date is set, and against all the odds Donna actually turns up, ready and willing to be filmed one last time. The set-ups are simple, I'll film the usual slow stripping around the house and a bit of bath-time action at the end of the day. Now, as you already know, Donna does not expose any of her pubic area. Her fans write in constantly looking for 'pussy shots' but there are none available. And of course there will be no such shots in her latest and final video, either. With this important knowledge on board, we sit down before we start filming and discuss how we can make Donna's video swansong her best ever, without her really showing much at all. It won't be easy, you know.

'How about nibbling on a banana, Donna?' I suggest.

Donna tells me she doesn't eat bananas, as they make her feel funny.

'Well, what about grapes?' my sister asks. Yes, Donna will eat grapes. And biscuits, she likes biscuits too. Half an hour later I'm filming Donna lying resplendent on a giant sofa, in some fine purple underwear, looking like a Greek goddess eating grapes. Or at least, trying to eat grapes. She's not very good at it, unfortunately, and most roll away from her mouth. So we cut, change food and move on to sexy biscuit eating. She starts with a Hobnob. It crumbles badly as it enters her mouth and most of it ends up on the floor or down her cleavage. In the end, we have better luck in the bathroom, where she doesn't have to eat anything. The finished video goes on sale a few weeks later and her adoring fans lap it up. Well, most of them do.

102

> I have just sent
> £15 POUNDS FOR yOUR
> PUSSy hair but forgot to
> send my address. Here is
> is.

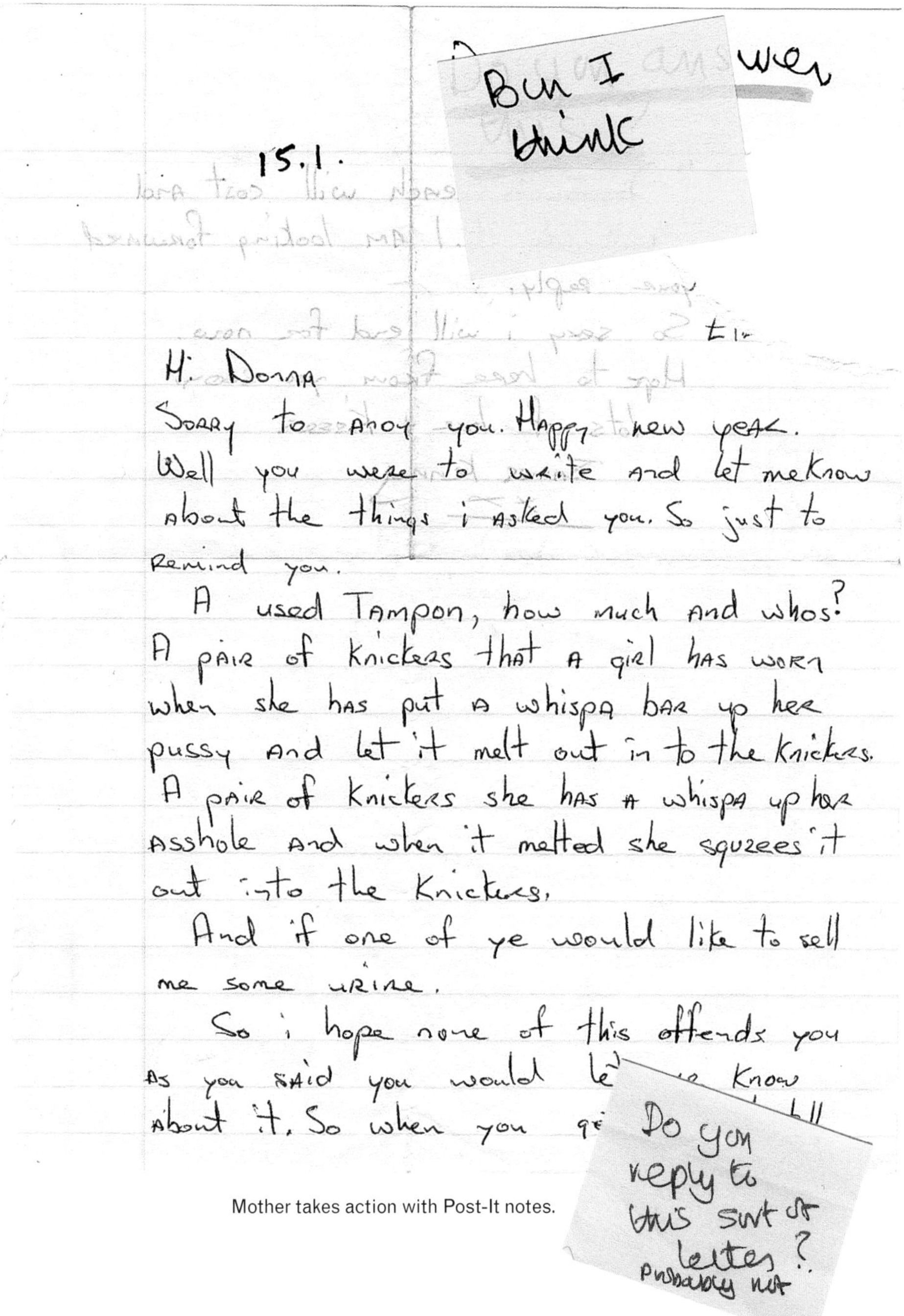

Bu I think

15.1.

Hi Donna

Sorry to anoy you. Happy new year. Well you were to write and let me know about the things i asked you. So just to remind you.

A used Tampon, how much and whos? A pair of knickers that a girl has worn when she has put a whispa bar up her pussy and let it melt out in to the knickers. A pair of knickers she has a whispa up her asshole and when it melted she squzees it out into the knickers.

And if one of ye would like to sell me some urine.

So i hope none of this offends you as you said you would let me know about it. So when you ge

Do you reply to this sort of letter? Probably not

Mother takes action with Post-It notes.

Mem No D214

Dear Donna

I received your Video today and I thought it was pathetic are you embarrassed as you cover yourself up all the time only knockers. Behind on veiw was wrong with the other bits. If it wasn't for the tape base I might have thought you were a feller in drag with implants I have noticed even on your photo you alway cover yourself whats worong with it does it go crossways or something If so I like to hear you slide down a bannister Rail. Also if you can not find your mouth with a cockay what can you find your mouth with. As to you shaving you didnt have to shave under your arms, the way it was mentioned in your ad It was a least a Bikini line (poor show) so come on lets see what you have got. I tell you

2

I will show you mine if I can see yours
In fact I saw more when I was at school
than I saw on your very short video.
I cannot believe you are embarrassed
I bet you see more in the back of a Taxi
than on your tape. If you were to come up
here were the scenery is fantanstic I live
alone except for a K9 and I could teach
you Advanced Timing allthough I dont
think I would get very advanced with you
you would be covering up all the time
and I could give you a proper painless
shave with clippers that vibrate nicely
and then finish off with a rayor to make
you smooth & kissable as I am 100% hetro
and like kissing beutiful things
        By the way what is continental on
your tape I was under the impression it was
open wide and if it your rudest yet I dont wish
to see the others.
                    Yours Sincerly
                                    D.

Not a happy punter. Not happy at all.

105

MEET THE GIRLS
— *Part Two* —

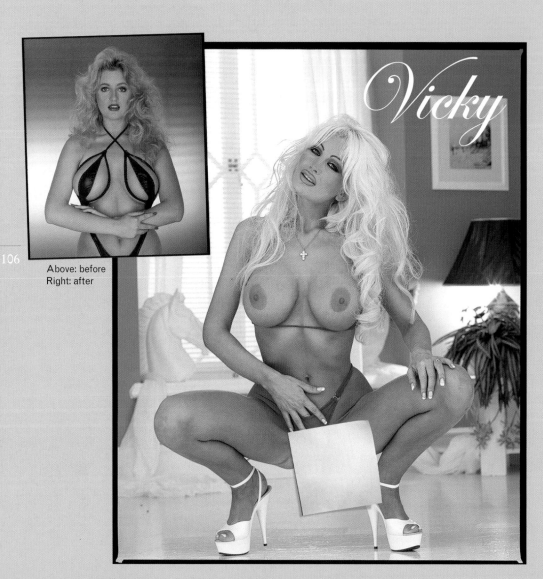

Vicky

Above: before
Right: after

106

Teresa

Lana

Alison

Belinda

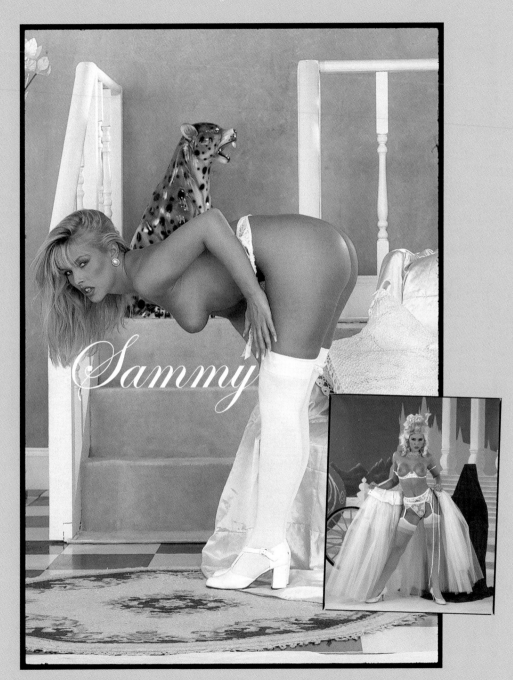

Sammy

Adele

110

Linsey

14

ALTHOUGH BY THIS point we're selling quite a few videos, there's an even greater demand for something a little stronger. From the letters coming in it's plain to see that men are buying the videos, enjoying them, and then writing back to ask if there's any chance of anything a bit stronger. By law an 18 certificate video is all we're allowed to make and sell – and by choice, too. We're a little old fashioned at the Fan Club – we don't do hardcore.

Nevertheless, hardcore is what's wanted, and things are changing with the BBFC, the Classification Board. The big chief has decided that we're all grown up in this country, and that we can now buy hardcore pornography – as long as it's consensual, normal, non-aggressive hardcore sex. So the Restricted 18 (or R18) category is created, and within a few months about seventeen hardcore videos have been passed in the UK. They're all American films, I think, one being a porno take on *Batman*. These videos are only available through the hundred or so licensed sex shops spread thinly around the UK, but the hardcore ripples have started, and Fan Club buyers soon realise they could get all the naughty videos they really want from elsewhere. Suddenly they no longer have to bother with our tame softcore, and there's a slow but very noticeable change in our video sales.

Further evidence of the rise of hardcore hits me later in the year when I work with a few of the Fan Club girls at the Erotica Show at Olympia – London's first ever major show for the sex industry. It's massive and people are excited, as you'd expect. It's two huge floors of everything to do with sex, with a special area devoted to domination, right in the middle. Every day for three days two of the Fan Club girls meet me at the Private stand, next to which is a giant 20-foot-high shot of my naked sister. We meet and greet men, take topless pictures for a tenner and generally have a fun time watching all the dressed-up sex freaks and show-offs walk past. It's a sex show and so about 50% of the punters who come wear their sexual tribal colours. There are women dragging men about on leashes. There are women with their pierced tits out. Rubberwear, piercings, erotic tattoos ... And lonely men everywhere. The Private stand we're working on is massive, the biggest at the show. If I remember right, Private is the organisation who managed to get the notorious *Batman* hardcore film passed at the BBFC. Anyway, before the show opens I meet the girls, Shanine and Lana. We prepare ourselves for the day ahead and I check all the cameras, film and Fan Club leaflets. The doors open. The sex rush starts. Obviously there was some information swapping going on in the queue outside as immediately everyone seems to know that this Private stand is where they can legally buy hardcore. It's so busy that after the first morning they've already sold out the stock they'd brought for the entire three days' trading. I've never seen anything like it in my life. Also on the stand are several full-colour TV monitors, playing a short loop of the videos on sale. Some of this is hardcore, and all legal. These monitors are man magnets. There is pushing and shoving, and I stand there watching crowds of punters transfixed by these looping hard images. I get a nudge from Shanine. She gestures towards a man to our left. He is a young man, maybe 25, maybe 30. He's standing there wearing a beige mac with his hands in his pockets. He is sweating and flushed. He's obviously wearing his special beige mac with holes cut in the pockets as the front of his jacket is moving in a filthy way while he watches the sex unfold on screen. We have him removed from the stand.

For the rest of the day we play cat and mouse with the fair organisers. Wherever you look there are topless women, porn stars and even hardcore porn on TV screens; there's even a very rude erotic dance show every couple of hours. But even with all this going on, the show organiser says we are not allowed to take topless pictures of the girls with punters. He says he has no licence for this. The girls and I all take turns trying to convince him we are doing nothing wrong, but he's having none of it. Nobody wants pictures with glamour models who aren't topless, of course, so when we can get away with it, business is brisk. By day three Olympia has turned into hell – I can take no more. But hardcore made a huge impact very quickly indeed. I have a feeling that sex in the UK will never be the same again. As the show finally wraps up I manage to blag a free Private T-shirt, which I continue to wear anywhere that grannies go shopping.

15

THE ANTIQUES WORK and Portobello still continue. The dealers I know are intrigued by the porn I'm involved with – especially when I wear the Private T-shirt. I get them free sexy pictures sometimes, which brightens their grey early mornings.

Antiques, records and porn … For obvious reasons I'm quite confused. I have no idea where to jump full time, which trade or work to really plump for. But things are changing. Even with all fourteen Fan Clubs going I notice a decline in the amount of post coming in. It's not a massive drop, but stock levels aren't quite as large as they used to be when we began. Instead of assembling seventy-five new Fan Club packs in one go, I'm down to maybe five. Some of the girls, like Vicky and Lana, get hardly any post at all; one letter a month if they're lucky, and even that's probably from Geoffrey.

There aren't too many good new models in the business either, so there are no new Clubs on the horizon. We need something new. Something different for the fans. Something exciting for them, other than photos, mags and undies. We've done videos to death but we haven't done sex toys yet, so we decide to give it a go.

The main trade distributor for all these rubbery sex objects is a funny old warehouse in an industrial park on the east side of the North Circular. Called Sheptonhurst, it's not for the general public; more like a giant Toys R Us for kinky adults. Row upon row, shelf upon shelf of videos, mags, huge wobbling dildos, funny rubber knickers, kinky outfits, edible oddities, things to sniff and rub on – if there's something you want, it's here in bulk and in every colour imaginable. I drive to this warehouse with Eve on a recce, to see what delightful sex toys we can supply to the fans, but it soon becomes clear that there's not much mileage in the new idea. Mags are boring and anyone can buy them at the local newsagent. Girls can't really sell dildos to men. Well, I suppose they could, but … In the end we're left with a few basic and obvious choices: blow-up dolls and glass bottle things with pumps attached you stick your knob into. And rubbery, sticky cock rings. So we choose the right kind of dolls, enlargers and rings for the Fan Clubs and then set about working out how exactly to sell them to all the fans. A few weeks later and out flies a new little self-penned leaflet with Fan Club Special Sex Toy offers all over it. Eve doesn't want to rip anyone off, and so prices for all these hideous sex treats are unbelievably cheap. You can get a doll for a mere £25. Cock rings – if you have any idea what they're actually for – are just £1. You can even buy this thing called an 'Oral Stimulator' for a tenner. It's a glass tube with a rubbery end and a pump-looking thing attached at the other. There is a shot on the front of the box of it in full use, but I have no idea what kind of thrill or job it performs. Anyway, the response is immediately good. We sell lots of dolls, and many fans buy two. Unfortunately there is no black blow-up lady doll, so the Charmaine fans will just have to go without. When the first shipment of dolls arrives at the Fan Club office my mother is in fits of laughter as I explain to her exactly how they work. My mother has never seen a blow-up doll before, and these are very funny to look at. They have 'real hair', in blonde or brunette. This is like soft fibreglass and is already tied into fat plaits with cheap red ribbons on either side of the dollies' flat, round heads. The boobs are like these solid domes with bullet nipples. I don't even bother looking at the dollies' nether regions and neither does my mother.

115

When it comes to shipping off these dolls to the eager fans, we have a slight problem. The trouble is, the doll boxes are just too large and square to get into even the largest Rhino bags we have, so each doll has to be lovingly taken from her box and then placed (not forgetting her mini vibrator and free lubrication) into the Rhino bag with some cardboard slotted in to protect her sides. When the bag is done up ready for posting, if you're not careful you end up with a sealed bag with two very obvious boobs and nipples poking into the Rhino bag surface, which looks kinky, strange and a little embarrassing when I drop them off at the post office. As I say, these dolls sell well, and I'm really surprised to find out how many of the older fans start buying them. I mean, I know exactly why they are buying them, I'm just surprised how many of them do so.

So the dollies sell well, and so do the funny knob toys. I don't really understand these. Luckily one fan buys one and then sends in a series of explicit shots (taken in his shower cubicle) of him in action with the toy. Yes, it obviously works on some levels, but I still don't want one. We also run a line of 'Real Pussies'. They cost about a tenner and for this tenner you get a blue box which says 'Real Pussy' on it, with a picture of an 80s-style naked bird on the front. When you open the box it's this kind of pink rubbery guessing game with two little holes in it. I don't think this needs explaining any further but luckily for us they are small enough to fit into the Rhino bags without having to be removed from their horrid blue boxes.

All these sex toys sell quite well, but it's just a short Fan Club fix really. In order to grow further my sister needs a new and reliable revenue stream, and it's not long before she hits upon another great Fan Club idea.

She rings her usual contacts and starts a new line selling classic Page 3 pictures. Not real Page 3 pictures that appeared in the *Sun*, just topless photos of the famous girls from the 70s and 80s who appeared in that paper. Good idea, methinks. So we start selling photos of Sam Fox, Linda Lusardi, Kathy Lloyd, Tara Bardot and literally hundreds of girls I have never heard of before in my life. Look down our neatly prepared list of vintage topless sex photos and you'll find some real treats: Lola Ferrari, the tragic cosmetic nightmare who sadly committed suicide; Colt 45, who has a 45-inch chest; lots of exotic-sounding girls with no surnames like Zita and Inga; and many more besides.

Now, I'm put in charge of all these vintage shots, but it's a sod of a line to run properly. If I have a run on one particular girl (let's say Linda Lusardi) and then order too many of her pictures, I can guarantee that the run will stop and the piles of new Linda Lusardi photos I now have in will never sell, or at least take months upon months to sell. My sister will spot we've got loads as she never misses a trick, and she'll wonder how on earth I managed to get so many Linda Lusardi shots and not have any buyers for them and then complain that I'm useless and just wasting money. And of course when I order too few of one girl (it always pays to be cautious, don't want any excess waste blah blah) and they all sell out, I then find myself stuck with no shots, outstanding orders waiting and then I find out that the photographic printers have lost the original tranny and it all goes tits up. This whole new job is an endless unpredictable nightmare for me and I don't like it at all. Christ, I should have a real bloody job by now, I shouldn't be putting old photos of Sam Fox in new envelopes for middle-aged men, should I? This is not the reason I left advertising, is it? Nice pictures, though, some of them.

But this new photo line Eve starts is still not really enough. Yes, lots of orders come in but there is definitely a dwindle in the Fan Club trade, and I blame the internet.

Almost overnight, computers are cheaper to buy and use, and home internet usage is up and growing by the day. We get letters from punters wanting to know when on-line versions of the clubs will open. Some even write and say they've made an on-line site for the girls already. Most larger sex organisations are already cashing in, but lots of our punters are old-fashioned, they still use pens and paper, they don't have computers, and they like writing in to the girls, not emailing them. We carry out surveys to find out if they want on-line Fan Clubs, and most say no. Personally, I quite like the all-new internet. I strike a deal with my sister and she allows me to get on with a Fan Club website, and even allows me to pocket any revenue after expenses and royalties are paid. I contact Derek – that's Dirty Derek, the web master. Within a few weeks a glamorous sex website is started for the Fan Clubs – it's an electronic paradise of sex, where you can see disgustingly high-resolution close-ups of all your favourite girls, and can even email them your fantasies. The site is impressive, glossy, sexy and very easy to navigate, and when it is launched from the next Fan Club mailing I sit there at the computer and wait for a stream of emails from the thousands of on-line fans. Not a dickie bird. One email from a geezer for Shanine, if I remember right, wondering when she was going to do hardcore. Nope, the internet was not for us.

Dear Eve
        Just a line to say that valentine card was very good I have marked off 4 with a tick for £20
        have you got something to pump up Doll as I have not got much wind to Blow it up thank you. from ████████

We started selling dolls, older men bought lots.

Dear Louise Darling.
          First of all I must tell you that I have been ill
since April 3rd but glad to say I am feeling better now.
     Thank you for my goodies, but I am sorry to tell you that
the Louise Doll when I blow it up the air comes out again I
found out this week which is a week later that the seam has
come apart, so I can't use it now to take you to bed with me,
now I will have to get another one from you darling.
     I know I just keep getting filthier and a dirty old man.
I know I am a dirty old man and I love it all. I will be
watching out for your Video so I can watch it.
     The Louise Doll is nice and Fucking Sexy, you have a nice
Sexy Bum, and a lovely Cunt, your Tits with erect nipples
and I could have buried my stiff Prick in your mouth until I
Spunked down your throat till you swallowed it, then I would
▬▬▬▬ Fuck your Spunky Cunt, then you would lie on your back
and you would put your legs on my shoulders and I would bury
my stiff Prick deep into your Spunky Cunt.
     This is only a short letter to let you know that the Doll
is faulty.
                    Love and Kisses
                      your dirty old man
                      and SPUNKY
                      Arthur.
                      ARTHUR.
               XXXXXXXXXXXXXXXXXXXXXXXXXXXX

DEAR LOUISE
PLEASE WOULD IT BE POSSIBLE
IF YOU COULD PLEASE SEND ME
TWO LOUISE BLONDE RUBBER
DOLLS THE TWO LOUISE BLONDE
RUBBER DOLLS I WOULD LIKE
ARE IN A BAG WITH A NEW
VIBRATER THE LOUISE BLONDE
RUBBER DOLL HAS LIFE LIKE
BLONDE HAIR AND THE BLONDE
HAIR IS TIED WITH RED

RIBBONS THE TWO BLONDE
LOUISE RUBBER DOLLS I WOULD
LIKE HAVE THE BLONDE HAIR
TIED IN TWO PONYTAILS AND
TIED WITH RED RIBBONS I
HAVE ENCLOSED £50 POUNDS
TO PAY FOR THE TWO BLONDE
LOUISE RUBBER DOLLS PLEASE
COULD YOU SEND ME THE TWO
BLONDE LOUISE RUBBER DOLLS
AS SOON AS POSSIBLE PLEASE
FROM YOUR NUMBER ONE FAN

XXX

PS THE BLONDE LOUISE RUBBER DOLLS
ARE IN A BAG WITH A VIBRATER WITH
EACH BLONDE LOUISE RUBBER DOLL
YOU BUY

16

AS MY SISTER says, the post is getting 'desperate'. A desperately small amount, I think she means. But even so, I still find a letter good enough to collect from time to time. I still have absolutely no idea what to do with the piles of porn letters I now have resting and recuperating at home. They sit in my room in boxes and files, and I always have a few in my bag. I know deep down something can be done with them, and I strongly believe they need to be seen, read and understood by others. I just have no idea how to work it yet.

One evening I'm headed for home after the porn work. I end up going to the boozer first, to meet a good friend of mine known as Wisbey – we haven't seen each other for a while and we intend to have a catch-up of sorts. He's living in my old flat in Chiswick. He's an actor, and he drinks quickly. We get pissed and talk about all sorts of rubbish, before going back to the old flat for a few more drinks and maybe a quick drunken look at *Star Wars* so we can recite all the lines as usual. It's something we never tire of. If we don't watch *Star Wars* it will be *North By Northwest*. Wisbey is currently going through his Cary Grant phase – by which I mean he is learning Cary Grant. Wisbey is a talented actor, musician and a genius mimic. Once he decides he wants to be someone he will study that person for months in order to get their accent and mannerisms just right. And right now, Wisbey is in his *North By Northwest* phase as it's when Cary Grant looks and sounds his best. So we get back to the old flat, I feel faintly nostalgic as we sit there drinking and talking, but then all of a sudden, looking through my bag for my roll-ups, I notice my porn-letter folder. This will be funny, I say to myself. I pull out the dog-eared pink file, grab a letter, hand it to Wisbey and ask what on earth he makes of it ...

Without batting an eyelid, Wisbey starts to read this letter out in the style of Cary Grant. It's perfect: the letter acts like a twisted script, an insane sexual monologue brought to life by a Hollywood star. I fall about in fits of laughter, reach into the file and pull another new letter out. I hand it over. Wisbey looks, thinks and then reads this out as a slightly strained toothless pensioner.

Eureka! I could be Rex Harrison in *My Fair Lady* singing 'By George I think she's got it' as Liza Doolittle cracks the accent. Here, in this grotty old flat, we stumble upon the key that unlocks all these little letters. It's simple: I have all these letters, Wisbey has all these voices. Put them together and the letters are brought to life. It makes them listenable, acceptable, even though the content is sometimes distasteful. It just works. We spend the rest of the evening trying different letters and voices. It's funny, sometimes hysterically so. It really does work. The next day I am unbelievably excited. I phone up Wisbey's brother, also known as Wisbey, and ask for his help. I have a plan. I want to record a selection of letters with his brother reading them out. Wisbey's brother is a sound engineer and radio studio manager – he understands sound and agrees immediately to help record us.

A few weeks later we find ourselves in a posh studio that we've managed to blag. We have about two hours on the free clock but we don't need it. I choose eight letters, Wisbey reads them out in different voices, sings two with his guitar and we're out of there in thirty minutes flat. I take the recording and decide to make and press a little 7" vinyl record with it. I call it 'Dirty Fan Male'. I press a few hundred, with sleeves designed by Dirty Derek, drive the records to my distributor and wait a few weeks to hear if people out there find the record (and therefore the letters) as strange, entertaining and thought-provoking as I do. I don't have to wait long. The little record sells out quickly. I go to record shops I know and already the staff behind the counters are repeating some of the phrases that appear on the record: 'My special message penis' and 'By a thursday' start to become part of their everyday language. Not what I expected at all, but a fine, fine result all the same.

It's time I think about trying a whole album of letters. And why not? The single has done well, sold out, created ripples of its own, so a date is set. I get together with Wisbey a few times to rehearse and talk about new letters I've found, we blag the studio again and record a further forty letters. 'One take' Wisbey doesn't fluff a thing and we are done in less that two hours. Some of the letters are simply read in accents ranging from James Mason to Obi-Wan Kenobe. Letters written in a noticeably poetic, rhythmic style are sung in a traditional folk-tinged fashion. Wisbey also does a mean Paul McCartney impression. He has perfected it over the years, mainly because he is a huge Beatles fan. I find a poem entitled 'I want to hold your hand' that was recently

121

sent to my sister. Wisbey performs it as Paul McCartney, but in his Wings period. Inspired. Hilarious. Filthy. Brilliant. And sad.

I sit on this recording for a bit. I want to release it to the world but just don't have the time to sort it all out and give it my full attention. It's also an album, which is very different from a simple insignificant 7" record. For a start, much more money is needed to make it, fund it, promote it. As an album it needs to appear in proper big record shops, but because of the explicit nature of the material some of the big shops can be a bit funny. They happily sell explicit hip hop, but draw the line at letters written to porn stars as read out by Kenneth Williams. So I just need to think about it all and save up enough money to get it moving properly.

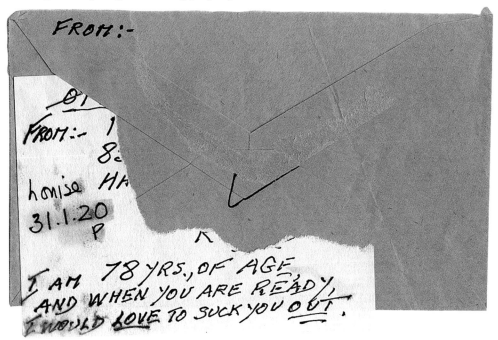

Letter no. 2 for Wisbey – read out like a toothless pensioner.

13.7. $34.95

DEAR MISTRESS LOUISE

        I AM A PERVERT. I LOVE TO BE DOMINATED BY BEAUTIFUL WOMEN LIKE YOURSELF.

    MY FAVOURITE IS TO PAY A WOMAN TO PULL MY NIPPLES HARD WHILE I WANK MYSELF OFF OR FOR HER TO GRAB MY BALLS AND SQUEEZE THEM UNTIL I GIVE HER MORE MONEY.

    I WOULD LOVE TO KNOW WHAT YOU WOULD DO TO ME IF I WALKED INTO A ROOM NAKED AND YOU WERE IN THERE WITH YOUR FRIENDS.

    PLEASE CONTACT ME IF I AM WORTH IT.

DEAR LEAH HARPER!

I WOULD LIKE YOU TO SEND ME PHOTOS AND A VHS VIDEO OF MYSELF COMPLETELY IN THE NUDE. I CAN NOT BE WEARING ANY BIKINIS, O-STRING BIKINIS, SWIMSUITS, SHORTS, LEATHER SHORTS, PANTS, JEANS, SHIRTS, T-SHIRTS, THONGS ATHLETIC T-SHIRTS, TANK TOPS, BRAS LEATHER BRAS, PAJAMAS, DRESSES, BABY DOLLS, STOCKINGS, TEDDIES, GARTER BELTS, SOCKS, LINGERIE SEE-THRU LINGERIE, LOUNGEWEAR, SEE-THRU LOUNGEWEAR, AND OTHER FORMS OF CLOTHING, LINGERIE AND LOUNGE WEAR IN FRONT OF AND COVERING MY TITS, NIPPLES, PUSSY, PUSSY HAIR, LEGS, AND FEET. I CANNOT HAVE A SHAVED PUSSY BECAUSE IT IS NOT LADY-LIKE TO DO. I CANNOT HAVE MY HANDS AND THE HAIR FROM MY HEAD IN FRONT OF AND COVERING MY TITS, NIPPLES PUSSY AND PUSSY HAIR. I SHOULD SPREAD MY LEGS APART TO SHOW MORE OF MY PUSSY AND PUSSY HAIR. I CANNOT BE WEARING ANY HIGH HEEL SHOES AND HIGH HEEL BOOTS BECAUSE I CAN HAVE FEET PROBLEMS LATER IN MY LIFE TIME.

I SHOULD TELL THE
MEASUREMENTS OF MY TITS
WAISTLINE AND HIPS IN
INCHES. CAN YOU SEND ME
THE PHOTOS AND VHS VIDEO OF
MYSELF COMPLETELY IN THE
NUDE BY A THURSDAY BY THE
BRITISH POSTAL SERVICE AND
THEN BY THE UNITES STATES
POSTAL SERVICE PRIORITY
MAIL.

SINCERELY YOURS

The first letter shown to Wisbey ... 'by a Thursday'.

1.0. No
money

27/9/99

Dear Sir,

I write to you in the <u>strictest Confidence</u>
I joined the <u>Donna Ewin Fan Club</u> in
June, but I was not sent the full
membership Pack. I assume you know about
me, but you need to understand what the situation is.
    In '95 I had a vivid dream that I am
to have a mystical Experience. My name
will Change to Don Male and lead an
important Campaign. I become London Male
my Active Force is PowerDon. My dreams
tell me to make Preparations.
    In '96 I have a dream that I am
to get my Soulmate, then I hear a name;
DONNA EWIN, I have never heard that
name before. I find out she's a model,
it leads me to the Sport and when I
see her, I look exactly like her.
    For Confidentiality I cant send a Photo in,
but <u>I will</u> Get a Glamour Model to see me soon.
    I start having dreams about her, I know
Lots of Personal things. I've Given
these dreams to the Sport and apparently
they are all true.
    I've also found out she's been made
the 'body' <u>and</u> an Escort, that she
is a Martyr. There are 9 boyfriends,
she likes them but it is abuse, she
actually cheats on them. She is not happy.

126

There has been a misunderstanding with
the Sport about my address. I will explain.
I am still living here with my Parents,
In a house. When I rang the Sport, they
asked me If I had a Garden. How can I
confirm I live here. The problem is I cannot
come in yet. I come in, in around 6 years time
thats the appointed time. If they find out
I live here, how can they keep me quiet;
The Top Male Model Britain will ever see,
They will knock on my door, So I had to lie.

We can meet right now, but we
cant get together.
I hope I've tried to make everything clear
All I can do now is stay by her side,
So its important you send these newsletters.
Can you please do me another membership
Pack, and I didn't get the last
Newsletter. I would be grateful if you can
Send any Past Newsletters and anything
about her. I think her starsign is
Virgo, the Virgin; cleansiness, she has
to have those characteristics
Please Reply Quickly, Please Realise that
If Im her Soulmate and these things
are not sent then for me its sad.

Yours Sincerely

███████

Don mail: recorded for the CD.

DEAR SHANINE

I AM A HIYNOIDE
ENGINEER. AND HAVE BEEN WORKING ON
THIS ROBOTICS. PROJECT SINCE 1988
OF ALL THE GIRLS I HAVE LOOKKED AT.
YOU ARE THE MOSTE BOUTIFULL! AND THE
NEAREST. TO WHATE I AM WORKING ON
AT PRESSANT. I AM WILLING TO PAY
MORE THAN THIRTY FIVE POUNDS. FOR
MORE ACCURATE INFORMATION ABOUT
YOUR FEATURES AND BODY. MY BIRTH
DAY IS 12/10/55 HOPE TO
HEAR FROM YOU SOON MISS
GOD BLESS

TEL

128

DEAR SHANINE

I HOPE THERE IS SOME
MONEY LEFT OVER.. FROM THE CHEQUE I
HAVE ENCLOSED. FOR SOME CHOCCOLATES FOR
YOU MISS. IF AT ALL POSSIBLE FOR MY
ROBOTT LADY ART FORM, OR YOU. I NEED
TO KNOWE YOUR HIEGHT LEG LENTH
INSIDE LEG. WIDTH ACCROSS THE SHOULDERS
I ESTAMATE BY MATHS RATIO YOUR FACE
TO BE 6 3/4" HIEGH 2 1/4" BETWEEN YOUR
PUPILS IES SET FORWORD. THANK YOU
FOR GOLD CLUB MEMBERSHIP AND THE
LOVELEY PHOTOSES. LOVE ▮ X

Dear Louise

I belong to your fan club. I was reading in the news of the world that kirsten Imrie was sleeping on park benches in london. I dont know if its true. But I would like to offer kirsten somewhere to live. I live in a 1 bedroom Council flat and I work as a Care assistant in ████████ There would be no strings attached and she dont have to have Sex.

Kirsten Can sleep on my Couch when I am off work and sleep in my bedroom when I work nights. Kirsten Can stay as long or as little as she wants. The only thing kirsten would need to do is feed my Cat when Im at work.

Kirsten have probably had plenty of offers. But I would like her to know there are people who Care. I would be very greatful if you Could Somehow get this letter to her.

Kirsten Can phone me anytime on my mobile if she wants a chat.

yours Sincerley

████████████████████ .

129

Dear Sharine Darling
Yes Summer's here at last, the time for
wimbledon, tennis, and Strawberries and
cream, i am a great fan not of
tennis, but of Strawberries and cream.
So here it goes i imagine a hot
Summer's day and you invite me for
a game? tennis that is, and you
know that i would play any game
wilt you.
Well we play tennis and to cut a
long Story Short we get all hot
and Sweaty who cares who won,
but suffice to Say after the game
we Slowley undress ourselves you take
my clothes off and i take yours off
Starting wilt your top, then your lacey
bra Slowley letting your wonderful tits

P.T.O.

free your Entire body glisens with sweat so i caress and lick your luscious tits this by the way takes some time, then i remove your skirt revealing white frilly lacy tennis panties, which by now are soaking, not just with sweat, so i take my time to remove them with my teeth, while also inserting my fingers in your fanny.

Then i lick you to your first orgasm of the day and drink down your heavenly juice, ooh did i say something about strawberries? well who needs them when i'am slurping on your creamy cum finally we fuck, you suck my cock, and we end up on the floor in a sweaty embrace, lots of love Shanine Yang.

Yours

Always

131

22/11/20. 05

DEAR ALISON

HELLO, I HOPE YOU ARE WELL AND FEELING SEXY

I HAVE RECEIVED MY FAN CLUB PACKAGE, SORRY IF I WAS A PAIN
WRITING TO YOU ABOUT THE PACKAGE. I AM HAPPY NOW.
I WOULD LIKE YOU TO KNOW A FEW THINGS ABOUT ME IF YOU
DON'T MIND ALISON. I AM 35 YEARS OLD, 5FT 8IN 12½ STONE
SHORT HAIR THIN ON TOP. I MAKE UP WITH A HAIR BODY AND MY
FRIENDS THINK I AM GORILLA. I AM SHY AND QUIET WHEN IT
COMES TO CONVERSASTION, THAT'S WHY I AM ALWAYS LAST IN THE
QUEUE. I WORK ON THE RAILWAYS HAS A VAN DRIVER (YOU CAN PULL
MY GEAR STICK ANY TIME AND FILL ME UP). I DELIVER STORES TO
THE SIGNAL BOXES, YOU CAN HAVE A RIDE IN MY VAN ANYTIME.
I HOPE YOU DON'T MIND ME WRITING A FEW SEXY SUGGESTIONS ABOUT
THE PRIVATE PHOTOS YOU SENT ALISON. THE PHOTO OFF YOU
PEELING OFF YOUR TIGHT LITTLE DENIM HOTPANTS WANTS ME TO PULL
MY TROUSERS DOWN AND SHOW YOU MY DELIGHT I LOVE YOUR
SMILING HAPPY FACE, AND I LUV LONG BLONDE HAIR. I WOULD LUV TO
LICK THOOSE GREAT NIPPLES THEY ARE LIKE TO CHERRIES WAITING
TO BE EATING. THE CABERAT PHOTO IS REALLY HOT, I BET YOU
COULD SHOW ME A FEW TRICKS. NICE TO SEE YOU WEARING BLACK
SILKY STOCKINGS, I WOULD LIKE THOOSE THIGHS ALL DAY. I WOULD
LIKE TO PUT MY TOOL BETWEEN YOUR BOOBS. ALL IN MY DREAMS
OF COURSE.
I WOULD LIKE TO ASK A FEW QUESTIONS IF YOU DON'T MIND
WHERE DO YOU COME FROM?
WHAT ARE YOUR VITAL STATISTICS? YOUR HEIGHT?
YOUR FAVOURITE COLOUR?
DO YOU HAVE ANY HOBBIES?

132

27.8.10

I WANT TO HOLD YOUR HAND.
I WANT YOU IN MY SLEEPING
                        LAND
I WANT TO KISS YOUR PARADISE
                ENTERANCE
I WANT YOU GIVE ME YOUR
        FULL SEX FUCKING
                EXSPEARANCE

I WANT TO EAT YOUR EATABLE
                BODY.
I WANT TO TJUCK A BITE
        LICK YOUR TITS
I WANT TO BE PLEASED LIKE
        NO OTHER BODY
I WANT TO TAKE YOU IN AND
        OUT OF EVERY BITS
I LOVE YOUR VERY FREE
        TO SEE BEAUTY
I WANT YOU TO BE MY CUTE
        TART SO FROUTIE.

Perfect for a McCartney pastiche.

133

To: Louise Hodges.

Dear Louise Hodges,

[Hello my name is Mr ▇▇▇▇▇▇] I am writing this letter to you because, i would like to thank you for the 'photo's' you sent me. I would also like to meet you in 'Manchester' on Sat 1st July 2000. (about 10pm) out side ('Arndale' centre piccadilly manchester)

Please turn up with a short 'top' + Denim shorts + black rubber boots.

If you can bring 'Linsey Dawn mckenzie' that would be great.

Please write to me as soon as possible. Thank you!

Yours sincerly

▇▇▇▇▇▇▇▇▇

Mr ▇▇▇▇▇▇

I fancy you. I want to 'Fuck' you hard.

134

The girls did not go.

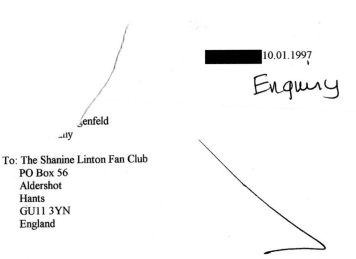

████ 10.01.1997

Enquiry

█enfeld
█ny

To: The Shanine Linton Fan Club
    PO Box 56
    Aldershot
    Hants
    GU11 3YN
    England

Dear Ladys and Gentleman ,

I found your adress in the Magazin " FOOTSY" .I have very much interest on all productions with woman feets . I collect everything from feets : Photos,Videos,Magazines....
For this reason i like to order by you.
I´m very Happy if you inform me what for products,prises and how i can order this products by you.

135

Whis very well greatings ,

████████

I hope i hear from you in the next time, because i have big interesting on your products!!!

6-12

Darling Veda,
Just to thank you for your video and stockings I love your video it is so horny I have had a good wank over it. I love the stockings also I keep wearing them I went shopping with them under my jeans yesterday they make my cock rock hard when I wear them. All my love and I hope you have a Sexsational Christmas.
Love

XXXX

17

MEANWHILE, BACK AT the Fan Club, the post is down more than ever. Many of the girls are winding up their porn careers now that hardcore is the order of the day. If we are to continue making videos we have to make hardcore ones in order to compete, but none of the Fan Club girls would be into that. Besides, hardcore is full of very different-looking women. They tend to have more spots. My sister also has a young family now and this is not the kind of business she really wants to get involved with, so things are changing here. With the post in terminal decline and the revenue dwindling away to nothing, my sister makes a decision: she decides to slowly wind down the clubs. Bearing in mind we send sales and newsletters out and some don't come back for at least two years, it will take at least 12–18 months before the mail stops coming in, but we'll tell all the fans now and they'll have a nice amount of time to buy and collect everything they want from the girls. At last, I think to myself, I have some real news for the newsletters. I type this all up with a surprising amount of joy, and these last fourteen newsletters all go out as the next and final mailing. Hundreds of sad letters all come back, mainly from the serial writers like Geoffrey, who write individually to all the girls with the same message.

It's not that sad for me. I've been sitting there in the office stuffing envelopes with dollies and mags wondering why on earth I am still doing this porn lark, and now an end is firmly in sight. I begin to think about making more records, and hopefully finishing this Dirty Fan Male thing I've quietly started. Within a few weeks Mr Dixon packs up his antiques stand in Portobello Road for good, so in the space of about three months I go from having three part-time jobs to no job at all, apart from dabblin' in the record business. The time is right now to start turning this little *Dirty Fan Male* recording into an album of sorts.

I enlist the help of Devious Derek (aka Dirty Derek), who has recently designed and assisted me in constructing a website for the records I produce. He loves women with their clothes off, he loves all the Dirty Fan Male letters, and it's really his enthusiasm for the whole Dirty Fan Male project that fires me on. Weeks go by and Derek slowly assembles a suitable cover for the album, a montage of hundreds of letters, all put together in a computery fashion. His attention to detail is almost perverted. Why am I not surprised? He places a Mr. Mason rose on the CD surface. I am pleased and excited. I decide to go ahead and make the album. It's not cheap. I invest all the money I have in this new devious baby of mine.

Nothing is ever simple. I remember the brief problems I had getting the Mary Millington record into shops, and so I have to get 1,000 'Parental Advisory' stickers made to go on the front of the new CD. All very tedious. A few more weeks go by and the brand-new, full-colour CD, complete with thirty-nine filthy and bizarre letters, arrives. I am as thrilled as I am apprehensive, and find myself saying 'What the hell have I done' a lot. Derek is just thrilled and enthusiastic.

Right. Next thing I have to do is set about selling the little buggers. I have to put some kind of press campaign into operation. I can't afford an expensive press plugger and there really is no point in getting a radio plugger on board as the content is a little too rude and explicit for radio airplay. So I assemble a list of suitable magazine and newspaper journalists, and get going. I send out about fifty copies of the brand-new CD (complete with Parental Advisory stickers) and wait for some enthusiastic responses. There are none. Bugger all. Nothing happens. My distributor is disappointed – no press reviews means no orders for the CD in big shops. The daring and fearless little independent music shops take a few copies, but I have no larger order from major shops. I'm gutted. I have about 1,000 copies of this all-new bloody CD that I love, and no one wants it.

So what do I do? I find my hero Oliver Postgate, the creator of some of the finest children's TV known to man, and get him to allow me to release *The Clangers* soundtrack on CD instead. I do it with knitted covers and it sells rather well, which makes up for the massive disappointment of the *Dirty Fan Male* CD.

Back at the ranch, the Fan Clubs are all winding down very quickly and relatively cleanly. I go in to work and there is no work. Or what little there is takes me about an hour to sort out. I realise how great this is: my mother can get on with enjoying her retirement, my sister can get on with her family, and I can struggle on with my new life in music production.

The Clangers buys me a bit of time. I think about what on earth I can issue next as a CD that might sell, but then suddenly it all starts to change with *Dirty Fan Male*. Little by little press reviews begin to appear. Fans of the CD begin to email me. Wisbey goes to parties and people talk to him about it. Interest grows, and there seem to be more CDs floating around than I've sold as fans burn copies for friends and the recording slowly makes its filthy way around the country via bootlegging, a little like the rude *Derek and Clive* tapes that flew about in the early 70s. Meanwhile the real CDs suffer from the fact that most record shops do not stock it, and those that do, like HMV, don't know where to display it in the store. Think about it. Where do you put a CD of rude letters written to porn stars read out in different voices? In HMV it ends up in the Indie Rock section, under 'D' or 'Various'. So if you go to a shop to buy the CD, the chances are you'd never find it. I tell you, it's an uphill struggle, this music business.

Dirty Fan Male publicity keeps popping up in funny places. A good review appears in *Kerrang!*, the rock magazine. *Bizarre* magazine wants to write about it, as does *Ministry*, a house-music mag. *Arena*, that classy old ship for men, mentions it. *Loaded* magazine doesn't. Then I begin to get emails from abroad, from Italy and New York. Italian art-house articles appear that I can't read. New York *Tatler* writes about it. Some big radio station in Dallas goes nuts for it. The filth is obviously spreading of its own accord. Sales figures are still non-existent, but there's really no lack of interest. We then get a call from Barry 7. He's in a post-rock-electronic band called Add (N) to X. He's in charge of a night of organised strangeness at the V & A. He says the *Dirty Fan Male* recording has 'got legs'. He asks us to perform a live version of it at this art music night, and we say yeah, why not. A month later we are standing in front of an audience of pissed weirdos in the middle of the exquisitely tiled William Morris room at the back of the museum. I'm just standing there mute, handing letters to Wisbey who's reading them out however he pleases. It's all very unusual and a little surreal. People laugh. People are shocked. People scratch their heads. People want to read the letters for themselves. The same night we meet Alan Cox, who's come along to watch us. He's an acting mate of Wisbey's, and mature beyond his years. Alan takes us to the pub like a father figure. He goes on and on about what could really happen to this thing we've just tried to perform, the potential that's there. It's all very exciting, and a bit of a mystery to me. More people talk about it and start dropping the phrases from the CD into their everyday language …

A few mornings after the V & A gig, I get a text message from Wisbey. He's not the most communicative of thespians, so when a message of any sort comes in I take note.

According to Wisbey, the London DJ Danny Baker is playing our CD on his breakfast radio show. I like Danny Baker, so I call his radio station, get through to his producer and tell them that both Wisbey and myself should come onto Danny's show and talk about the CD.

They call me back within the hour and ask us to come in the next day, at 7.30 a.m.

The next morning we both arrive on time, and we steam into the friendly and almost chaotic live arena that is the BBC in Marylebone High Street. We spend about twenty minutes of the show discussing exactly what went on and how this devilish little CD came into existence. Danny Baker declares it a work of pure genius and the funniest CD he's heard in decades, and we are seriously taken aback by it all; everyone in the studio laughs all the time we are there and an hour later I get a call from the cowboys who run my website internet shop that CDs of the album are selling about one copy every ten seconds. It's going to be a grower.

18

MY LIFE FINALLY takes on an air of normality. Well, sort of. An email comes in from a journalist who's a massive fan of the *Dirty Fan Male* CD; he tells me he uses it at home like audio Prozac. When he's feeling down or if he's had a bad day he'll listen to it, and instantly feel better. His girlfriend doesn't approve. He believes it has huge, unexplored potential and suggests a visit to the Edinburgh Fringe Festival, not to sell the CD but to put a show on, using the letters. I decide to take it seriously and start talking to Wisbey. He's done Edinburgh before and is up for it again so I make enquiries and begin to research how Edinburgh works as a festival, how you can take part and exactly how you put on a show. Oh, and more importantly, how much it might well cost. It looks like a huge gamble, and will cost both time and money that I don't really have.

First things first, you need a venue. But even before that, you have to join the Fringe as an organisation in order to find out what venues are around. I muddle through it all, and with the help of Wisbey and our new theatrical director, Alan Cox, we plump for any tiny venue that will have us. After pitching our show to all these tiny venues, we sit back and wait to find out if they'll have us. My pitch is a simple letter and a copy of the CD.

Two weeks later and to our huge surprise we have our first-choice venue all lined up. They really want us. We say yes. Things look good already. Over the next few months I have to complete various Fringe tasks, like organising and paying for flyers, paying for mandatory advertising and finding grotty cheap accommodation for the three *Dirty Fan Male* heroes in the city of Edinburgh. For once in my life I am disgustingly organised and get it all sorted out very quickly, and well in advance of any deadlines. So, the stage is set – we are going to perform *Dirty Fan Male* at the Edinburgh Festival. This coming August. And it's already July. Erm, and we haven't got a show yet. We've had one meeting in the pub six months ago, during which we all got pissed, didn't talk about it at all, and spent most of the meeting watching Alan Cox womanise.

With the big month approaching fast I call an emergency meeting. We all agree that another actor is needed on stage with Wisbey to talk about how the recording and letters came about. We need a narrator and a narrative. The idea of Wisbey just endlessly blurting out letters is not a show and will not make theatrical sense. I have no proper stage experience except for dressing up as a gypsy woman in the play at junior school, but I volunteer. Alan makes it all sound terribly easy, sends me off to write the narrative and a date is set for first and final rehearsals a week later.

A week later, and we converge on the Actors' Centre, a large set of theatrical spaces a short luvvy hop from Shaftesbury Avenue. We have a rehearsal planned but it turns into a full first run through in front of an audience that somehow Alan has dragged from nowhere. I am horribly nervous, I was expecting a rehearsal in front of no one. I don't know the script and any preparations I have made were not with an audience in mind. I find it all unbearable and embarrassing to start with. I read from index cards I've written out, Wisbey performs from the letters and an hour or so later the small and unexpected audience stop laughing. It's very obvious even though this first run-through is chaos that something is working with what we've quickly cobbled together. I imagine more run-throughs, more rehearsals, but there are none to speak of. Instead, we have two very live performances two days before the Edinburgh trip kicks off, in a real theatre space in front of a larger seated audience. Again I am crapping myself, but this time I have prepared a little harder, I have learnt the narrative as well as I can, and we have prepared a series of slides showing my naked sister, the other girls from the Fan Clubs and a great shot of my pensioned mother wearing shades.

Again, we bumble our way through it all, there are several mistakes and the crowd's reception is surprisingly encouraging. At least, they laugh out loud a lot. This is all very good news as Edinburgh is less than seventy-two hours away.

Three days later and we're opening for the first time at the Edinburgh Fringe. Our chosen venue is a suitably seedy little cave just off the Cowgate, one of the larger, longer roads in the city centre. It seats about fifty, on little pews. When it rains outside, it also rains inside the cave. It's perfect for the forty-five minutes of porn letters and story we have ready for our small audience. We are supposed to spend the hours before the show (and every spare moment we have) handing out the show flyers I've had expensively printed. They are A5 in size, with a big pair of horrid knockers on the front. The flyers announce the arrival in Edinburgh of *Dirty Fan Male* and three large words are prominent on the flyer front: 'filthy', 'hilarious' and 'disturbing'. Two of these words cover up the nipples on the horrid boobs. We have about 2,000 of these flyers to last us the month. On day one we are too busy to give any out at all.

The first night brings us a good performance, a small enthusiastic crowd and a major critic. She hates it.

We haven't got a very big budget for our Edinburgh run, no big publicity machine behind us, no flashy fly posters, no agents, no pluggers; but like the original *Dirty Fan Male* CD, the show slowly starts to gain its own little momentum. We realise that people are talking about it, newspapers and Fringe magazines begin to write about it, favourable reviews begin to arrive from nowhere and our little cave gets busier as the days go by. Well-wishers, actors and comedians come up to us in bars to tell us how much they love what we've done. The month becomes a whirl of drinking, porn letters and laughter, we wake up singing or quoting from the show, and soon become known as the 'dirty boys' around the fringe venues and bars. Wisbey keeps the show fresh by changing some of his impressions, and when he hits upon a new voice for one of the more explicit letters the result is a show highlight for us, with Stan Laurel dreaming about 'tonguing Teresa May's bum crack'. This phrase quickly enters the pre- and post-show banter.

The show rolls on, Alan brilliantly re-directs us every night and gets us to push everything we do on stage. He misses nothing. Our audiences get bigger and better, as do our nightly drinking sessions. Every night the show begins at 7 p.m. (after Wisbey's final poo), and we get home at 5 a.m. Edinburgh is like a timewarp: bars don't shut, there are no clocks anywhere, and the days flow by on a river of drink.

We reach a pissed climax at the end of week two, where we all sit and wonder what the hell we are doing and why we've done it. We talk more about the letters: about the men behind them, and the fact that what we are doing has not really been done before; it breaks rules, crosses strange boundaries. Wisbey sits there, more pissed than normal, and confesses his sadness for it all. And it is sad. We sit there and agree, it's a comedy show all about sadness and loneliness. Every night Wisbey reads out these letters – real letters written by real people, some of which are quite tragic. The show is deliberately structured to make the audience both laugh and think about the tragedy and solitude behind the letters; nonetheless, it's like we are trading on this tragedy, and all of a

143

sudden we begin to feel uncomfortable about the whole thing. Wisbey smashes his favourite umbrella, and we all go to bed at dawn in a disturbed state.

The next day I get up and look at some new fan letters my mother has sent up as requested. They seem a little darker than normal and they start to spook me. I put them in the sink and burn them all, one by one. There are passport pictures of some of the fans in amongst the letters, pictures I've kept for years and not bothered about, but now they seem to stare at me. They know. I burn them too. It feels like a ritual or something, but burning those letters releases a huge amount of tension that has been building up inside me for I don't know how long.

My girlfriend arrives from London and we sit together in the festival flat, talking about the night before: the broken umbrella, our communal guilt, the madness and sadness we all now feel. The tragedy we're revealing, the audience laughter at it all, the exposure of privacy and the final paranoid burning of letters. I break down.

All the dirty boys meet for lunch and on reflection of the past weeks and last night realise that all three key words on the flyer don't just apply to the show, but also apply to the ride we're currently on. This is not what we expected at all.

We may be disturbed by it, but the show must go on. We still don't give out flyers but the show seems to work its own little magic, bringing people of all ages and from all kinds of places to our little cave. It's all out of our hands; more reviews appear and in most cases note both how funny the show is, and how uncomfortable. The show sells out.

By the end of the month-long run, we realise it's been incredibly successful (in a very small way) in a crowded and wildly competitive festival – there are 1,700 shows running at the Edinburgh Fringe this year, and we've done it all without the financial backing and promotion that tends to be required – we never did give out those flyers.

Almost as soon as it begins, our Edinburgh experience is over. Wisbey and Alan make their own way home and I throw the boxes of flyers in a skip when I've finished hoovering the flat for the first and last time.

I leave Edinburgh on foot, catch the bus near the big railway station and head for the airport. My flight is delayed, so I sit in the over-lit, fast-food-filled departure lounge and reflect on what a hedonistic, hellish washing machine I've been thrown about inside for the past month. I feel terrible. I've not eaten too well (but drunk far too well) for the whole of August. To pass the time I look at the glittering press we've received for the show over the last few weeks. Amazing reviews, endless praise and even an award. So we did it. We had a successful show, a word-of-mouth hit against all the odds.

We somehow pulled it off. All on our own. And I finally realise what has gone on in my life. There I was, only a few short years ago, leaving advertising because it wasn't a creative business, and here I am now, leaving Edinburgh knowing I've finally created something I can be proud of. It's all I ever wanted to do and I start to cry.

Which looks a bit shit in an airport departure lounge, unfortunately.

Pages 145-152 – new letters tried and tested at Edinburgh.

077

DEAR DAILY SPORT

PLEASE SEND ME TERESEA MAY FAN CLUB GOODIES UNDER DESCRIT PLAIN PACKAGING MY MOTHER DONT AGREE WITH THAT SORT OF THING.

MUCH THANKS

████████████

⑧

145

Dear whoever this letter conce..

I am putting this letter with the videos, because my son ▮▮▮▮ only recieved 6 videos and I was already sorting out prosedures to get them back to you because I do not keep that kind of filth in my home. You will not be getting any orders from my son any more. I would also like you to know that the cheques he has been using were from my cheque book. I hope this will be an end to the matter and I do not want to hear from you again

Mrs M▮▮▮▮▮

MONDAY
11 NOV 96

12/11/10   'PC
                    Panties —

DEAREST BELINDA!!
                    I THANK YOU FOR YOUR PACK;
I'VE STUDED YOUR PHOTO AND I LIKE WHOT
   I SEE.
      YOUR YOUNG + SWEETS — I RECKON
YOUR ABOUT 20 OR 21 YEARS OLD AND
36 × 34 × 36 — AM I RIGHT ??

YOUR EYEBROWS + NAILS ARE WELL KEPT, -
— I CAN SEE YOUR A CLEAN GIRL; —
— WHOT ABOUT YOUR RING — ARE YOU
ENGAGED - OR IS IT FOR THE SAKE OF WEARING
   A RING ??
YOU HAVE A LOVELY PAIR OF TITS AND I WOULD
   LOVE TO SUCK THEM.
   YOU SENT 8 PHOTO'S BUT NONE SHOW YOUR
   CUNT — BUT I HAVE NO DOUBT YOU HAVE
      A NICE PINK HOLE.
IF YOU DON'T WANT A 69 JUST LIE ON
   YOUR BACK — A PILLOW UNDER YOUR BUM
   FOR AN UPLIFT AND I WILL LICK YOU
OFF AND TASTE YOUR SPUNK — SHOULD
BE NICE WITH YOU.
      THROW YOUR CARES TO THE WIND DARLING —
YOU HAVE NOTHING TO FEAR FROM ME — I'M NOT
      A BLUE LAMP BOY — I JUST AN
   ORDINARY GUY WHO LIKES HER CUNT.

147

Dear Eve,

When I first joined your fan club a
couple of years ago, I didn't really know what
to expect. I'm glad to say that I haven't
been dissappointed (although I didn't realise
that you would be _that_ naughty in your photo's!).

I must say that I am not a big fan
of pornography, but I consider you to be more
an erotic model, rather than pornographic. I feel
this largely because it is you who controls
who see's what. Also your fan club is something
that is personal between you and your fans, there
is no publishing house getting rich from what
you do.

There aren't many people who could run
a business as successfully as you do. I think
this is one of the reasons which I admire
you so much. You obviously saw a business
opportunity and you grasped. I don't think I
would have the necessary skills to do it.

The other night I was explaining to
my girlfriend why I didn't think joining
your fan club was an abuse of women. She
agreed my points but stumped my argument
by asking what I knew of you personally.

It was then that I realised that I know very little. I hope you don't mind me asking you a couple of questions,

a) What is your favourite book?
   (and who is your favourite author?)
b) Who is your favourite musician?
c) Has anyone bettered Olivier's Hamlet?

Yours with best wishes,

149

██████████

P.S. Thanks very much for the Christmas card, and please find my order enclosed. I'm looking forward to my surprise gift!

My Darling Teresa

P.S Can I still get your worn panties like before?

In my dreams you have agreed to let me worship your lovely arse. You bend over and pull up your very smart skirt, part of your business suit, just like Hillary Clinton wears, to reveal very scantie panties under your sheer tights.

Just as I lean forward with my tongue out to start licking and sucking, you instruct me to stop, as you want to shit yourself first, before I start! Yes, right in your tights and panties! sigh.

LOTS OF LUST, xxx

13.11.10.05 *love & kisses*
P

My dear Sammy

I've only seen you on one video but already I am lusting after your gorgeous arse. I've already got all the videos advertised but I look forward to receiving your worn panties which I will lick and sniff while playing with my cock and dreaming of tonguing your bum crack. Yes I would just love to stick my tongue right up your arsehole. God I'm now wanking like fuck as I'm writing this, suck your arsehole oh God, watch you having a shit as you bend over in front of me, your arse only inches from my face.

Send Letter
Back
26/3/—

24-MARCH. 2001.

Dear Donna,

thankyou very much for my recent order, there is one thing i do have to tell you though; i really do like looking at you, you bring me a lot of pleasure, you see i like to look at beautiful things and lady's too, AND this doe's DEFINATELY MEAN'S you; your order has cheered me up no end, as i am recovering from a bad spell of the FLU, which for some UNKNOWN reason i seem to get at this time of year, AND with regard's to you calling me a SPECIAL FRIEND, for some reason or another all the people that i deliver mail to regard me in the same way, so i just wish i knew why.

i do like the photo's of you in the RED COSTUME, very sexy as you are a sexy lady indeed; anyway i will always be a friend to you, as outside of work i do not have any friend's as my job interfer's with the social side of life and the people i work with do not include me in there sports activetys as i think that someone at work has spread a nasty rumour that i am a Homosexual, i know i am not and i think you know i am not, as the (loops) i would like to have a wife and some children; i joined your FAN club because, 1, i LIKE the female of the species, 2, it is good for me to have communication with the opposite sex AND one last thing i will send you a photo of myself when my DENTAL WORK has been completed.

19

ONCE EDINBURGH IS well and truly over I have a little more time to reflect on what has gone on, and what we have created. We get invited to do a few more, longer shows, so I go to the box file in my bedroom and dig about a bit for new material. We try these new letters out live, and they all work well in the new extended show.

We perform a short run at the Croydon Warehouse Theatre, which seems a bit random but we do it all the same. The theatre is larger than the cave in Edinburgh, the audiences get bigger, and to our delight the show still works. We always believed, because of the nature of the show material, that it was best suited to a small, intimate venue, but it really cooks in front of a good crowd. One of the many visitors to our Croydon run comes all the way from Birmingham. He's a confirmed *Dirty Fan Male* fan, and tells us that the expression 'my special message penis' from the CD is common parlance where he comes from.

The Croydon run over, we organise a special one-off night back in London in my favourite venue, Bethnal Green Working Men's Club. This WMC has not changed since the 60s; it's huge, and smells exactly as you would imagine, of stale spilt beer and ciggies. Over the bar is hanging the message, 'Happy 60th Anniversary Fred and Ethel'. It's a great venue, like something out of *The Sweeney*. It holds about 200 people. We book the night and it sells out – it's our biggest ever show, twice the audience we have ever had. My mother and Eve also turn up to see exactly what I have been up to. The show is a huge success, and a man at the bar even wets himself. I hope it's just because he's been laughing so hard.

There is talk of a trip to New York with the show, and one to Australia. Theatres around the country are keen to put it on. Suddenly, out of nowhere, someone asks me to write a book about it all. Well I never.

Pages 154-159 – new letters for Croydon.

154

Dearest Louise,

      Queen of my darkest fantasies, mistress of the most hidden pleasures of immagination, at whose feet I prostrate myself, being my most secret whim to grovel and beg living only to fulfill your each individual wish hoping that one day you make play with your little dogs bone. (NUDGE, NUDGE, WINK, WINK!) After all was it not Prospero who said "We are such things as dreams are made of" (sarc. THE TEMPEST. WILLIAM SHAKESPEAR.)

      In my opinion your are truly the sexiest woman alive, who has lived and who ever will live, with whom very few can even compete Eve Vorley and Ada Garman being two of the only three the third being Jo Guest, but even these three beautiful women are nothing in comparison to you.

      Two things I wish to point out, I was orginaly somewhat slow in placing the

①

order contained herein, So I thought I would probably end up missing out on some of your pubic hair, therefore I decided to delay my order in the hope that some may have grown back, however if it has not, I would understand and hope you would send me something appropriate in its place (anything that you would choose I know would be an exceptionally sexy choice) therefore I would be greatful of such a choice!

Secondly I would like to point out than in my opinion no mechanical device could even come close to the thought of you sucking me off, despite what you say, just the idea is orgasmic.

In this order I'm really looking forward to both the photoset of you and Viola Carman, and the video of you and Eve Vonley as I have previously stated in this letter, these are two of the only three women who even come close to you, so to be able to have the ability to see you and these two ladies together is yet another one of my fantasies realized.

I would like to point out the amount I enjoyed my last order, to do so I would tell you the first time I watched Louise I thanked God that I'm ambidextrous as I

put such a strain on my right arm I
put it in a sling.

Incidentaly the reason I quote
Shakespear is that like we befound a dark
side to pleasure however although similar
in many respects we do have our differences,
for him the darkness was to dominate and
be in control at all times, with me, my
deepest darkest fantasy is to be dominated
and subjugated, preferably by you.

Written in love and subservience by
your eternal slave,

████████████████

P.S. Just to assure you I know you are
my fantasy and could never be my
reality

Summer Newsletter :- £97.00
Lesbian Juses :- £18.00
            TOTAL :- £115.00

③

2.   A classic. We begin on page 2.

letter. Until then, you will have to make do, with this letter and presents.

I hope you have a very nice Christmas, and go to parties, etc. Take good care, of your property, if you need to be away, even for a short time. Burglars and other thieves are particularly active at Christmas. If you leave your home, even for a short time, see that all locks are secure, the same with your car, and all the fundamental things are done, like cancelling papers and milk.

Also, at parties, if you get an opportunity to have sex, see a packet of four is in your handbag, even if you are on the pill!

Now, here are a few of my memories, to make you feel sexy and horny! Firstly, in the 1940's when I was about 17. I remember, an older man and a young man in a latrine, The young man had obviously had one of his first experiences of sex. The older man asked, DID YOU GET A NICE FEELING? Also, a year or two later, at an institutution, there had been a Ball. The, luscious, nurses had, and their admirers had had a good "FUCK IN" [Some years].

157

3.

Hypocrits, were SHOCKED, or JEAL
-OUS, because they had not been
able to get any of it! They said,
"FRENCH LETTERS ALL OVER THE PLACE
THIS MORNING!"

Some years later, in a park, 2 young
girls and two young boys, were sexual
fooling around, in a cricket pavilion
after dark. One, was obviously screw-
ing a pussy! He called out "alright,
"ALL RIGHT FRANK, I'M NEARLY THERE!"
One girl appeared to be lying on the
other one, she shrieked out, "HYACINTH
GET OFF ME".

I will close now, wishing
you all you would wish yourself

████████████

20

NOW I WONDER what I've really done here. Yes, it's a book, as requested – but it's not a diary. I think it's a memoir of sorts, although that sounds a bit grand for my scrappy, disorganised life. No, this book is everything I can remember, and I'm sure I'll recall lots more when it's off and being printed and it's too late to change anything. And there will be many days when I will wish I'd written it better or in a different style. But at the end of the day, this book is all about those letters that I collected because I believed they were too good to throw away. They are the most interesting letters I have ever read; terribly funny, yes, but also sad, tragic and touching.

I never wanted to work in porn – it just all happened and seemed convenient at the time. But it showed me exactly how that business works, and my attitudes to it changed completely. I realised it was a service industry: that there are tens of thousands of men who rely and depend upon it to get through their day, night or week. It gives pleasure to all these people, to men of all ages and persuasions.

And even though these letters are fairly recent, the late Nineties and early Naughties are already a bygone era of pornography, an age that has long since passed. People don't write letters any more, we all seem to send emails nowadays, and softcore has had its day. Hardcore is everywhere and appears in your inbox every day, whether you like it or not. The Fan Clubs were like a little old-fashioned business that gave a huge amount of pleasure for a few years to thousands of men all around the world.

As for the writers of these letters, well, to me they are heroes. It's hard to write down your feelings, especially your secret sexual feelings and desires, but these guys manage, quite brilliantly, to do so and in some cases say a huge amount with great economy. I really do admire them.

These letters offer a unique view of what pornography is all about, from the all-important and mostly forgotten point of view of the consumer himself. There are hundreds of TV shows and books about the sex business, the stars, the film-makers – but nothing about the men who really make it tick as an industry, those lonely men behind the drawn curtains in a house on a street near us all. And this is what this book and the show we have created are all about. To make you think for once about these men.

I have not tried to analyse what goes in the letters, what these people are like or in some cases how mad they appear to be. I have never passed judgement on any of them. Some can write well, some cannot. And whether they can or not is something I do not care about. The main thing is that they all try to express themselves, and all succeed. I leave it to you to draw your own conclusions and paint your very own pictures of them all.

And now this is all out of my system, I can hopefully pursue some kind of new and exciting career. Well, that's what I wanted to do in the first place.

Thanks for reading and entering into the funny little world I have paddled about in for the last few years. I hope you find the letters as fascinating and odd as I still do. And one final word: the old Fan Club PO Box is shut and has been shut for a couple of years now. From time to time, and whenever I remember, I will check with the postman to find out if anything has by chance come in. All I can say is that Geoffrey is still writing.

F I N

Strange Things We Were Sent
(& Other Ephemera)

This page:
Our Mother, the porn pensioner.

Facing page, above:
The Cat's Back in Putney. A life-changing boozer.
Facing page, below:
A young Eve, with a younger Jonny. She was good in front of the camera at an early age.

Location, location, location. From small flat to footballer's house and finally to an old barn. Fan club offices.

Look. Boxes and boxes and boxes of fans.

Trunk Records' first release.

A handful of classic Eve Fan Club videos. Note 'Swedish Sex Games' with Adele. Contains nothing Swedish and was shot in Essex. No games present either, but some naked hoovering.

29.12.12

QUEEN EVE
EMPEROR OF UNIVERS OF SeX
QUEEN OF BEAUtY iN UNIVERS

A unique and direct way of ordering. Game of Sex was not a big seller. It will not be mentioned again.

ChEQUE OF
NO "ᵒᵒᵒ133"
FOR ⟶

Geoffrey's 'big rising willie'.

Donna: Greek goddess and muse to Fan Club members

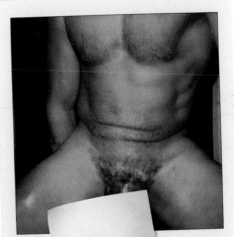

Above: Naked fan shots turn up all the time. Very few
manage to work out the flash in the face problem (but that's the least of their worries).

Above right: A special treat inside a birthday card to Eve. What a lovely suprise.

167

We get sent all sorts of things. Here someone has cut out a photo of Vida, then stuck it on his wall, and then
taken nine (yes nine) polaroids of it and sent it back to Vida. With no covering letter. We show only six here,
but you can imagine what the others look like.

The bleak hell that is the Circus Tavern. I don't want to go again.

168

Yes, all very disturbing in Edinburgh. Letters and fans' photos got burnt in the sink.

Oh how they danced. And caused fights. The Circus Tavern booted beauties on a big night.

Above: Look, it's a very rude vinyl record. Mary Millington talks dirty and wees.

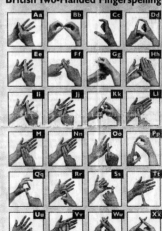

Right: A British sign language chart ... why?

The cult CD. 32 tracks in all. And with an eight page booklet.

The first Edinburgh Fringe flyer. Filthy, hilarious and disturbing. Exactly. (Art by Derek Collie).